BGP4

The Addison-Wesley Networking Basics Series

The Addison-Wesley Networking Basics Series is a set of concise, hands-on guides to today's key technologies and protocols in computer networking. Each book in the series covers a focused topic and explains the steps required to implement and work with specific technologies and tools in network programming, administration, and security. Providing practical, problem-solving information, these books are written by practicing professionals who have mastered complex network challenges.

Tom Clark, *Designing Storage Area Networks: A Practical Reference for Implementing Fibre Channel SANs*, 0-201-61584-3

Gary Scott Malkin, *RIP: An Intra-Domain Routing Protocol*, 0-201-43320-6

Geoff Mulligan, *Removing the Spam: Email Processing and Filtering*, 0-201-37957-0

Alvaro Retana, Russ White, and Don Slice, *EIGRP for IP: Basic Operation and Configuration*, 0-201-65773-2

Richard Shea, *L2TP: Implementation and Operation*, 0-201-60448-5

John W. Stewart III, *BGP4: Inter-Domain Routing in the Internet*, 0-201-37951-1

Brian Tung, *Kerberos: A Network Authentication System*, 0-201-37924-4

Andrew F. Ward, *Connecting to the Internet: A Practical Guide about LAN-Internet Connectivity*, 0-201-37956-2

Visit the Series Web site for new title information:
http://www.awl.com/cseng/networkingbasics/

THE ADDISON-WESLEY NETWORKING BASICS SERIES

BGP4

Inter-Domain Routing
in the Internet

John W. Stewart III

ADDISON–WESLEY

Boston • San Francisco • New York • Toronto • Montreal
London • Munich • Paris • Madrid
Capetown • Sydney • Tokyo • Singapore • Mexico City

Many of the designations used by manufacturers and sellers to distinguish their products are claimed as trademarks. Where those designations appear in this book, and we were aware of a trademark claim, the designations have been printed in initial capital letters or in all capitals.

The author and publisher have taken care in the preparation of this book, but make no expressed or implied warranty of any kind and assume no responsibility for errors or omissions. No liability is assumed for incidental or consequential damages in connection with or arising out of the use of the information or programs contained herein.

The publisher offers discounts on this book when ordered in quantity for special sales. For more information, please contact:

Pearson Education Corporate Sales Division
One Lake Street
Upper Saddle River, NJ 07458
(800) 382-3419
corpsales@pearsontechgroup.com

Visit AW on the Web: www.awl.com/cseng/

Library of Congress Cataloging-in-Publication Data

Stewart, John W., III.
    BGP4 : inter-domain routing in the Internet / John W. Stewart, III.
    p. cm.—(The networking basics series)
   Includes bibliographical references and index.
    1. BGP (Computer network protocol) I. Title. II. Series:
The networking basics series (Reading, Mass.)
   TK5105.555 .S74 1998
   004.6'2—dc21
                              98–44335
                                  CIP
                                 Rev.

ISBN 0-201-37951-1
Text printed on recycled paper.
3 4 5 6 7 8 9 10—CRW—020100
Third printing, June 2000

To my friend John E. Suich,
Who helped me love computers.

Contents

Preface

This book is about Border Gateway Protocol Version 4 (BGP4). At the time of this writing, BGP4, the latest version of BGP, has been deployed extensively on routers within the Internet. BGP is a routing protocol for the Internet Protocol (IP). A routing protocol is defined by a set of message formats for describing the reachability and preference for network addresses along with rules for processing information learned through these messages. The role played by routing protocols in networks is to ensure that information can be sent between computers connected to the network. For example, an individual dialing in to the Internet from home probably wants to access information, make a purchase, or communicate with friends or colleagues. These resources may be far away from the user's computer, and it is the routing protocols that are responsible for making sure that information can be exchanged between the user and the resources.

BGP is an *inter-domain* routing protocol. The Internet is a collection of many thousands of networks—from the largest backbones to the smallest dial-up providers and from multinational corporations to an individual dentist's office. Routing protocols are run completely internally to each of these networks as well as between a network and its neighbor. Inter-domain routing protocols such as BGP are the glue that ties the various networks together to make sure that a user of one network can reach a resource no matter where it connects to the network.

The number of people who either need or want to know about BGP has increased dramatically in the past few years, for two reasons. First, the growth in the number of Internet service providers has been explosive in the recent past. Second, many companies depend on the Internet for mission-critical exchange of information or for revenue stream either through Internet sales or through the sale of advertising space on Web pages. Such organizations often need to understand and use BGP either because of their sheer size or as a way of maximizing the efficiency or reliability of their Internet connection(s).

This book presents a practical introduction to BGP and is structured so that it can serve as a reference for people who need to use BGP. Chapter 1 gives an introduction to the TCP/IP protocol suite and to routing in general. Chapter 2 describes the protocol itself, including the messages and the rules for processing information learned through the protocol. Chapter 3 describes how BGP is used and explains the operational details that are important to know to use BGP. Chapter 4 describes the major extensions that have been made to the original specification to increase the protocol's usability, stability, and scope of operation.

The intended audience is people who have a solid understanding of general computing and at least a cursory familiarity with networks. The background presented in Chapter 1 is as brief as possible, although it attempts to give enough information so that someone who is not an expert in IP can understand the operational details of BGP as well as the reasons for some of the design choices. For readers who are curious about either TCP/IP in general, routing in general, or some particular area of BGP, the Appendix lists a number of references for further reading.

Acknowledgments

This is a short book, but it created more than its fair share of stress in my life for several months. Trying to tackle the project of writing a book for the first time shortly after moving across the country, starting a new job with a Bay Area networking start-up, and starting a new relationship certainly presented some challenges. Given this set of challenges, there are a number of people I need to thank for helping me start and, more important, finish the project.

First, I should thank Mary Hart (*nee* Harrington) of Addison Wesley Longman, Inc., who is responsible for the overall project. She was patient, persistent, and, amazingly, pleasant in her periodic requests for status updates.

Next, I should thank John Fuller of Addison Wesley's production department. He was extremely professional and reliable in seeing the book through to publication.

Next, I should thank Allison Mankin of the University of Southern California's Information Sciences Institute. Allison was my boss for a year and suggested to Mary Hart that she check with me to see whether I had an interest in writing a book on BGP. Allison has been a friend to me in many ways for most of my career, and I appreciate everything she has done for me.

Next, I should thank my professional friends and colleagues. It is certainly they, and not I, who are responsible for my knowing enough about BGP to write this book. My jobs at the Corporation for National Research Initiatives, MCI, USC/ISI, and now Juniper Networks, along with my associated involvement in the IETF, have given me a chance to meet and learn from some incredibly talented people. It's impossible to list everyone, but some of the people I'd like to mention are Roy Alcala, Tony Bates, Scott Bradner, Vint Cerf, Ravi Chandra, Enke Chen, Bruce Cole, Dennis Ferguson, Scott Huddle, Joe Lawrence, Tony Li, Allison Mankin, Yakov Rekhter, John Scoggin, Rob Sparre, and Paul Traina.

Next, I should thank the people who reviewed both the proposal for this book and an early draft of the full manuscript. Their comments were helpful and insightful and definitely improved the final product. Many thanks to Jeffrey Burgan (@Home Network), Joe Furgerson (Juniper Networks), Gerald L. Hopkins (Bell Atlantic), Barry Margolin, Robert Minnear, and Yakov Rekhter (Cisco Systems).

Finally, I should thank my family. My mother, father, and sister were very supportive, albeit from 3,000 miles away. My partner, Tim Houston, struck an unbelievable balance of encouraging me to keep working while simultaneously being a pleasant distraction. He dealt with my being absent for quite a while, and I really appreciate his patience.

John W. Stewart III
jstewart@juniper.net
San Francisco

1

Introduction

This book is about version 4 of **BGP** (**Border Gateway Protocol**). BGP is a routing protocol used in the Internet and, more generally, in internetworks based on **IP** (**Internet Protocol**). The material presented here is appropriate for people who have a fairly comprehensive understanding of general computing and some familiarity with the basic concepts of computer networking. Although this book could be useful to someone who wants to implement BGP but is not familiar with its use, it should not be considered a complete protocol specification. Implementers and particularly curious readers should consult the most current version of the protocol's specification for authoritatively complete information.

Until a few years ago, BGP was something known and used almost exclusively by a small number of large ISPs (Internet service providers). The engineering and operations staff within those ISPs understood BGP either because they were involved in the IETF (Internet Engineering Task Force) process, which specifies and standardizes Internet protocols such as BGP, or they were trained by someone in their organization.

Starting in about 1995 (the beginning of the popularity of the World Wide Web and, by extension, the Internet), however, the number of people and organizations that needed or wanted to understand BGP grew tremendously. There were primarily two reasons for this growth. First, there was a significant growth in the number of ISPs, many of which must use BGP to connect to other ISPs. Second, organizations came into existence that had a mission-critical dependence on their Internet connections, and those organizations often take great care in understanding all parts of the system to ensure the availability and performance of their connections.

Despite the dramatic increase in the demand to understand BGP, however, there has not been a corresponding increase in the availability of clear documentation. The IETF publication of the base specification of the protocol does not satisfy the need for tutorial information but instead is intended to ensure that independent implementations of the protocol interoperate with one another.

So the purpose of this book is to describe BGP clearly and completely. The approach is a practical one so that the book is useful to someone who wants to learn about BGP in general as well as someone who, for example, has a specific task to do and needs to learn about a specific part of BGP.

This introductory chapter includes the necessary background information for understanding BGP and the role that it plays in IP internetworks that use it. This background material has been kept to a minimum so that it does not get in the way of the usability of the book as a quick guide and reference; however, the background material presented here is considered essential to an understanding of the big picture of which BGP is a part. Chapter 2 discusses the base protocol in terms of the state machine, packet formats, and protocol rules. Chapter 3 deals with many of the practical details related to operating BGP. Chapter 4 deals with extensions to the protocol that either have been made or are being made as of this writing. In addition, Appendix A contains information for readers interested in finding out more about a particular area.

This chapter starts with a brief primer on IP and then discusses details about IP addresses and the need for routing. Following this, general routing terms and issues are introduced. Next, **CIDR (Classless Inter-Domain Routing)** is described. To set the tone for the ensuing detailed chapters, a high-level view of BGP is then presented.

1.1 A Brief IP Primer

Books such as this one often use the seven-layer **OSI (Open System Interconnect) model** of the ISO (International Organization for Standardization) to separate networking into several functional areas. The architecture created by the Internet protocols (primarily IP, **TCP**

[**Transmission Control Protocol**], and the applications), however, doesn't map well into seven layers. So instead we present the five-layer model shown in Figure 1-1.

The functions of the five layers are as follows.

Application This layer contains the protocols that directly serve the users. Examples are **HTTP** (**HyperText Transfer Protocol**) for the Web, **FTP** (**File Transfer Protocol**) for file transfer, **SMTP** (**Simple Mail Transfer Protocol**) for e-mail, **TELNET** for remote login, and so on.

Transport The Internet protocol suite offers two transport protocols—TCP and **UDP** (**User Datagram Protocol**)—each of which provides a different service. UDP, the simpler of the two, provides an unreliable, one-way, non-rate-adaptive mechanism for passing individual messages. UDP is useful for applications that involve the sending of a short query followed by the return of a short response.[1] If an application uses UDP and requires reliability, it must provide that reliability itself. TCP, on the other hand, provides a reliable connection between the communication endpoints, so it includes

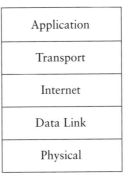

Figure 1-1 *Five-layer Internet architecture*

---

1. UDP is also used for *multicast,* in which there is one sender but many receivers. Even multicast applications that want reliability currently use UDP because doing multicast over TCP does not scale to support a very large number of receivers.

explicit acknowledgment, retransmission, duplicate detection, and so on. TCP also controls the rate of data transmission in order to maximize the user's performance without congesting the path through the internetwork. Both TCP and UDP include the idea of **port numbers** so that connections can be identified, both to set up the connection initially and to send a packet to an existing connection. For the host playing the role of the server, a *well-known* port number will be used (for example, TELNET's port number is 23, SMTP's is 25, and HTTP's is 80).

Internet This layer contains IP and provides the lowest layer of basic internetwork-wide reachability. As a result, routing is a function of the Internet layer. IP, like UDP, is a **connectionless** protocol, so each packet is treated independently. Another protocol contained in the Internet layer is **ICMP** (**Internet Control Message Protocol**). ICMP is used for diagnosis or for reporting status between network elements. An example of ICMP's diagnosis capability is the **ping** facility using the ECHO-REQUEST and ECHO-REPLY ICMP messages; it allows users to confirm whether or not they are able to reach a destination. An example of a status report capability of ICMP is the ability for a router to redirect a host to another router for sending traffic to a particular destination. This allows a router to optimize the path taken by the traffic if the host chooses a nonoptimal path.

Data Link This layer contains technology such as Ethernet/IEEE 802, FDDI (Fiber Distributed Data Interface), and so on. It basically represents the protocol "running on the wire."

Physical This layer involves the electromechanical details of **LANs** (**local area network**s) and point-to-point networks and their associated physical connectors.

In terms of operating system organization, application-layer programs typically exist as programs at the user level. The transport and internet layers are typically implemented within the operating system itself, and user-level programs make system calls to access the services. The data link layer is typically implemented between the operating system and hardware-related drivers. The relationship between these protocols is shown in Figure 1-2.

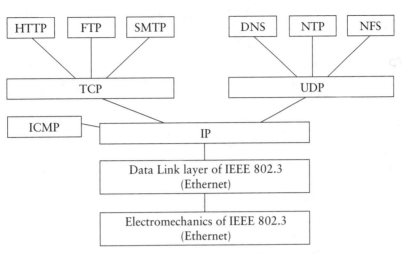

Figure 1-2 *Layering relationship between protocols*

The remainder of this section focuses on IP. The current version of IP in predominant use in the Internet is version 4.[2] As of this writing, the IETF is completing the specification of version 6 of IP, and some experimental deployment of IPv6 infrastructure is being done. Some mention of IPv6 is made later in this book, but the focus is IPv4, so unqualified references to IP should be assumed to mean IPv4.

IP is a connectionless protocol, meaning that it does not provide any kind of connection establishment. Each IP packet sent contains all the information it needs to get from the source to the destination. Conversely, **connection-oriented** protocols provide mechanisms to set up a connection between two nodes. With connection-oriented protocols, packets sent along a connection are identified by an identifier for that connection. As a result, intermediate nodes such as switches and routers can forward the packets based on the state set up during connection establishment. In the Internet architecture, applications that

---

2. The fact that the current versions of both IP and BGP are 4 is purely coincidental.

need rich services (such as acknowledgment of packets for reliable data flow and flow control for maximum throughput without congesting the network) get them from TCP. Applications that are satisfied with an unreliable connection with no flow control can use UDP. The advantage of this architecture is that the amount of state held in a router is a function of the number of nodes connected to the network and not a function of the number of user connections flowing through that node at any particular time. This arrangement makes the routers simpler devices than they would be otherwise.

One of the most essential pieces of any Internet layer protocol, both for routing and for the architecture in general, is its addresses. IP addresses are 32 bits long, so there is a limit of about 4.2 billion (2^{32}) on the number of possible hosts that can be supported.[3] In practice, the maximum size is probably lower because of certain requirements of the addressing system that must be met for the routing system to scale. IP addresses are typically written in **dotted-quad notation,** in which each of the four octets is written as a decimal number with dots separating the octets. For example:

10001010 00100111 00000010 00000101 = 138.39.2.5

A fundamental part of the IP architecture is that individual interfaces—and not whole hosts—are the elements that are addressed. This means that a host that, for example, has two interfaces connecting to two different LANs is known by at least two different IP addresses. For this reason, routers, which typically have many interfaces, are typically known by many addresses.

Note that IP has knowledge only of addresses and not *names*. An application layer protocol called **DNS (Domain Name System)** maps variable-length ASCII names (for example, www.ietf.org) into 32-bit binary IP addresses. The point is that this mapping happens before data is handed to IP for transmission, so IP never sees the DNS names.

Figure 1-3 shows the diagram of an IP packet.

---

3. The number 4.2 billion considers only "pure" IPv4 and does not factor in technologies such as NAT (Network Address Translation), which may be able to support a larger Internet.

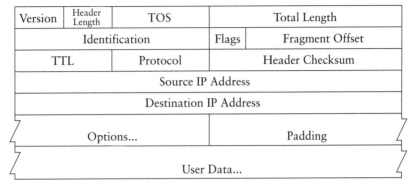

Version	Header Length	TOS		Total Length	
Identification			Flags	Fragment Offset	
TTL		Protocol	Header Checksum		
Source IP Address					
Destination IP Address					
Options...			Padding		
User Data...					

Figure 1-3 *IPv4 packet*

The meanings of the fields in Figure 1-3 are as follows.

Version This 4-bit field identifies the version of the IP specification to which the packet is formatted. As mentioned earlier, the current version in predominant use in the Internet is 4.

Header Length This 4-bit field specifies the number of 32-bit words in the packet header. A typical IP packet header has a length of 20 octets, meaning a Header Length field of 5, although if the packet contains options it could be longer.

TOS This 8-bit field specifies whether the packet should receive any special *type of service*. This field has been largely unused in the past. In recent years there have been a number of proposals for ways to use this field to support different levels of service within IP. The Differentiated Services group of the IETF is working on a new standard for this part of the IP header. The current specification for the TOS field splits it into two subfields plus two unused bits:

  D/T/R This 3-bit subfield can specify the combination of special treatment that the packet should receive with respect to *delay, throughput,* or *reliability.*

  Precedence This 3-bit subfield specifies a strict priority of the packet relative to all other packets (the priority is absolute and not, for example, relative to other packets from the same source).

  Reserved These 2 bits are reserved for possible future use.

Total Length This 16-bit field specifies the number of octets in the packet, including the header.

Identification This 16-bit field is used as an aid for reassembling packets. If a router needs to send a packet on a particular link but the packet is too large to send as one unit on the link, the router can break the packet into smaller pieces. For the receiving host to be able to reassemble the fragments back into a whole packet, the fragments must all be associated with the same packet. The Identification field provides that feature.

Flags This 3-bit field is used as control for fragmentation. The leftmost bit is reserved and should be set to zero on transmit and ignored on receive. The middle bit is the DF (*don't fragment*) bit. If a sending host doesn't want a packet to be fragmented, even if that means that the packet can't reach the destination, it can set this bit. If the bit is cleared, routers are free to fragment the packet. The rightmost bit is the MF (*more fragments*) bit. When a router breaks a packet into some number of fragments, all fragments except the last one will have the MF bit set. The last fragment will have the MF bit cleared. This arrangement indicates to the receiving host, which must reassemble the packet, that the last fragment has been received. Note that, because IP packets can be reordered or lost, the fact that the last fragment has been received does not necessarily mean that all other fragments have also been received.

Fragment Offset This 13-bit field identifies the location of this fragment in the whole packet being reassembled. This field is measured in units of 8 octets.

TTL This 8-bit field is used to control the length of time that a packet stays in the network (*time to live*). When a router forwards a packet, it is required to decrement the TTL field by at least 1. If a router receives a packet that has a TTL value of 1, the router should drop the packet and send an error message to the source. This field ensures that traffic doesn't get stuck in the network in the event of a forwarding loop.

Protocol This 8-bit field indicates how to interpret the data portion of the packet. Most often, this field identifies an IP packet carrying either TCP or UDP.

Header Checksum This 16-bit field provides a hop-by-hop check that the previous link or router did not corrupt the packet header. The checksum field is computed as the 16-bit one's complement of the one's complement sum of all 16-bit words in the header. For purposes of computing the checksum, the value of the checksum field is zero.

Source IP Address This 32-bit field specifies the IP address of the end node that sent the packet.

Destination IP Address This 32-bit field specifies where the packet should be delivered. The most common type of destination address is a **unicast address**, in which the address indicates the single interface to which the packet should be delivered. Another possible type of destination address is a **multicast address**, in which the address indicates a multicast group and, by extension, the set of interfaces to which the packet should be delivered. The final type of destination address is a **broadcast address**, which is used to deliver a packet to all IP nodes on a particular network.

Options This variable-length field is used to specify any options associated with the packet. The vast majority of IP packets in real networks do not contain options. Some examples of options are to record the route taken by the packet ("record route"), record timestamps from each router visited (timestamp), specify a "loose" source route by specifying one or more routers that the packet must transit on the way to the destination ("loose source route"), or specify a "strict" source route by specifying every router that the packet must transit on the way to the destination ("strict source route").

Padding This variable-length field is used to ensure that the header length of a packet with options still is a multiple of 4 octets.

User Data This variable-length field contains the higher-layer protocol, typically a TCP segment or UDP packet.

1.2 Notes on Terminology

As in all other fields, the words used to refer to concepts and to describe operations about routing are important. Because routing itself is not a mainstream topic, there is not a mainstream vocabulary that can be assumed. Rather than describe concepts using terms that are inaccurate or rarely used in the real world of networking, an effort is made to use the correct words starting at the introduction of a new topic.

Many networking terms are used casually, and the result is a partial or incorrect understanding of the underlying concept. This section introduces a few of these terms that are important for understanding the content presented here.

The first terms are *host*, *router*, *end node*, and *intermediate node*. A **host** is a computer whose primary use is directly for an end user or as some kind of server (file server, Web server, and so on). As for networking, the important point is that all the traffic arriving at a host is intended for that computer and not for some other device. A **router**, on the other hand, is used primarily for forwarding traffic between networks; so most of the traffic arriving at a router is actually intended for other nodes, and the router's job is to forward the traffic closer to the destination. The terms *end node* and *intermediate node* are a little less absolute. These words often refer to the role a device plays with respect to a particular flow of traffic. Specifically, in a unicast exchange, there are two **end nodes** and any number of **intermediate nodes** that participate to get the traffic forwarded from the source to the destination. The subtlety here is that, in some instances, a router can be an end node. Consider an instance in which someone from a **NOC** (**network operations center**) remotely logs in to a router to diagnose a problem using an application-layer protocol such as TELNET. In this situation, the two end nodes in the TELNET flow are the host in the NOC and the router itself. The important point here is that routers are not always intermediate nodes for all flows and can actually terminate an application-layer connection themselves.

Another pair of terms that are often used interchangeably, even though they have distinct meanings, is *routing* and *forwarding*. Understanding the difference between these terms requires understanding the underlying way that IP works in getting data from a source through some number of intermediate nodes to a destination. The next section goes into detail about the low-level mechanics, so at this point we'll look at only a small amount of abstract information. For every node in a network to be able to exchange traffic with every other node, the intermediate nodes between every possible combination of endpoints must know the direction to send the traffic so that they can get the traffic closer to the destination. A given intermediate node's understanding of the topology can come from sources such as static configuration and dynamic routing protocols. It is possible for an intermediate node to have more than one path for reaching a particular destination. For reasons such as choosing the optimal path and choosing a path consistent with administrative or technical policy, it is necessary for an intermediate node to analyze the information it receives from its various sources and select the paths it wishes to use. This decision process is called **routing**. A **routing table** is used by an intermediate node to help it make its routing decisions. A routing table inside a node typically includes all the information that the node knows about the topology of the network in terms of links and locations of destinations. After all necessary decisions are made about which path(s) to use, if any, a **forwarding table** is created. When a node receives a packet on an interface, it looks up the destination address in the forwarding table and *copies* the packet to the interface that gets the packet closer to its destination. This act of receiving a packet, doing a lookup, and copying the packet is called **forwarding**.

In the past year or two the term *switching* has begun to be used synonymously with forwarding. Traditionally, the term *switching* was used to refer to the forwarding of layer 2 frame and cell technologies such as Frame Relay and ATM. There has been a perception that technologies such as this were fundamentally faster than IP, so applying the word *switching* to the act of IP forwarding implied some kind of speedup. This text will use the term *forwarding* rather than *switching*.

One final note on terminology involves one of the most frequently used words in this book: **network**. In the real world of IP networking, the word *network* is used in two primary ways. The first and probably most obvious definition is an infrastructure of links and routers. The other use, though, is to refer to a particular group of IP nodes that have related addresses. For example, saying "network '18' is used by MIT" doesn't refer to a physical network but instead refers to issues of addressing. In the current Internet, the term **prefix** is synonymous with this latter definition of network, so this text will try to be consistent and use the term *prefix* for clarity.

1.3 IP Addressing and the Need for Routing

To this point, IP addresses have been discussed in a relatively abstract way. This section gets into more detail about the relationship between addressing and routing.

Figure 1-4 shows three Ethernet networks: Ethernet 1, 2, and 3. Ethernet 1 has two hosts and one router connected to it, Ethernet 2 has one host and two routers, and Ethernet 3 has one host and one router. Hosts A and B can exchange IP traffic directly over Ethernet 1 without needing to use a router. Hosts A and C, on the other hand, can exchange IP traffic only if Router 1 forwards that traffic between Ethernets 1 and 2. This direct versus indirect connectivity is something of which the hosts themselves are aware because, for example, Host A behaves differently when talking to Host B versus talking to Host C.

Because a host must behave differently depending on whether or not the destination is directly connected, it obviously must know

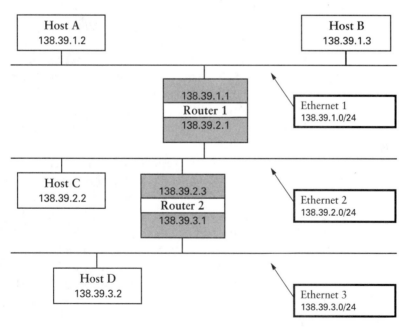

Figure 1-4 *Example topology*

which situation it is dealing with. If the destination is directly connected, the sender will send traffic directly to the destination. If the
sender is not directly connected, then it consults its forwarding table to
see the intermediate node to which traffic toward that destination
should be forwarded; the assumption here is that the intermediate
node (for example, Routers 1 and 2 in Figure 1-4) will take responsibility to forward the traffic closer to the destination.

The way that a host knows which situation it is dealing with is
based on the addressing. Two nodes that are directly connected have
addresses that have some number of leading bits in common. Conversely, two nodes that are not directly connected do not share the necessary number of leading bits. The number of leading bits that must be
in common depends on the **mask** of the network to which the node is
connected. In Figure 1-4, the network represented by Ethernet 1 is
138.39.1.0/24; in other words, all interfaces connected to Ethernet 1
will have addresses whose first 24 bits are 138.39.1. So, for example,
Host A's address is 138.39.1.2 and the router's interface on Ethernet 1 is
138.39.1.1. The configuration of each interface on a given node
includes, at minimum, the address and mask of the network to which
the interface connects. When a node has a packet to send to a destination, it finds the number of bits in its mask and compares that number
of leading bits in its address and in the destination address to see
whether the address fragments match. If the fragments match, the
nodes are directly connected and can send traffic directly to one
another without having to go through a router. If the fragments don't
match, the nodes cannot directly communicate and instead must send
traffic to an intermediate node that will forward the traffic toward
the destination.

The exact way that a node compares the leading bits is to use a 32-
bit representation of its mask, do a binary AND between that and its
address, and compare that result to an AND between its mask and the
destination's address. The 32-bit representation of, for example, a /24
mask contains 24 1 bits in the leading part of the address. For example, the comparison Host A would make when sending a packet to
Host B is shown in Figure 1-5.

Another example, shown in Figure 1-6, describes a comparison for
Host A and Host C, which are not directly connected. Because they are
not directly connected, Host A will forward the traffic intended for

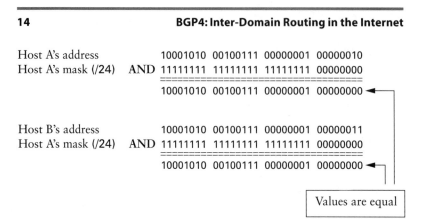

Figure 1-5 *Comparing Host A and B addresses*

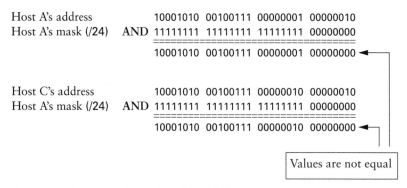

Figure 1-6 *Comparing Host A and C addresses*

Host C to Router 1, and Router 1 will forward that traffic directly to Host C via Ethernet 2.

The example in Figure 1-6 shows how Host A learns that Host C is not directly connected, but that step is only the beginning of the process that results in Host A's packet being delivered to Host C. Once Host A knows that it cannot deliver the packet directly, it next must decide the **next hop** to which it should deliver the packet. The term next hop will be used often in this text and simply refers to the node that gets a packet closer to the intended destination.

In practice, deciding the next hop is accomplished in one of four ways. First, a host could be statically configured with a **default router** (an address of a directly connected router to use for all destinations not directly attached to the host). A second option is to use a dynamic protocol between a host and some server on an attached network. An example of such a protocol is **DHCP (Dynamic Host Configuration Protocol)**, which can perform a number of tasks, including assigning an address and DNS name to a host as well as assigning a default router, DNS server, file server, and so on. The advantage of using a protocol such as this one is that you can make network configuration changes by changing a database on the DHCP server instead of having to go to every single node on the network. The third option is to use a protocol specifically for **router discovery**. Extensions have been made to ICMP that add router discovery functions to IP, although it isn't very commonly used in practice. The fourth option is to have a host participate in the routing system itself and exchange routing information with routers. In this last case, the host will have a dynamic forwarding table of its own. Although this approach is sometimes useful for complicated hosts (such as ones that have multiple interfaces on multiple networks), such a configuration typically involves more complexity than necessary.

So at this point, through some mechanism, Host A has decided to use Router 1 as the next hop for reaching Host C. The result is that Host A forwards the packet to Router 1's Ethernet interface on Ethernet 1. Note carefully that the destination IP address of the packet is Host C and *not* Router 1. Upon receipt of the packet, Router 1 first sees whether the packet is actually intended for local delivery (for example, if the packet is part of a session for someone logging in to the router itself) by checking the destination address of the packet against all its interfaces. Note that this comparison of destination address against interface address must compare all 32 bits of the addresses. In this case the packet is not intended for local delivery and instead is a transit packet, so Router 1 must make a forwarding decision. This forwarding decision is exactly the same as the decision made by Host A when forwarding the packet along the first hop. So to be precise, Router 1 receives a packet addressed to **138.39.2.2** and must decide where to send it. The only difference between this and the decision made by Host A is that Router 1 has more than one interface.

However, the forwarding decision generalizes nicely, and Router 1 simply checks the destination address of the packet against all the networks to which it is connected. Because Router 1's interface on Ethernet 2 (address 138.39.2.1) and Host C's interface (138.39.2.2) have the leading 24 bits in common, Router 1 knows that it can forward the traffic directly to Host C over Ethernet 2. After Router 1 does this forwarding and Host C receives the packet, Host C will compare the destination address against its interface address and see that the packet is intended for local delivery. At this point, Host C will pass the packet to higher-protocol layers in the operating system (for example, TCP if the packet were part of a TELNET session logging in to the host).

One final scenario with respect to Figure 1-4 is Host A wanting to reach Host D. This case starts in the same way as Host A wanting to reach Host C and remains the same until the point that the packet reaches Router 1. When the packet is received by Router 1, Router 1 again sees that the packet is a transit packet and not one intended for local delivery, so Router 1 tries to make a forwarding decision for the packet. However, without additional information not shown in the diagram, Router 1 cannot make the forwarding decision. This scenario is a good example of the usefulness of dynamic routing: if Router 1 and Router 2 exchanged routing information and let each other know the networks to which they were attached, Router 1 would be able to see that Router 2 is connected to the 138.39.3.0/24 network and would forward the packet across Ethernet 2 to Router 2's interface on that LAN. From that point, Router 2 would be able to forward the packet based only on the addresses and mask and not on any dynamic routing. Without dynamic routing protocols to communicate this information, it would be impossible to manage large networks because a huge amount of static information would have to be configured into every node in the network. This scenario is particularly true under failure conditions, when traffic may need to take paths that, under other situations, would be less optimal.

In summary, when a host sends a packet to another host, it either sends it directly to the destination or to an intermediate node for forwarding closer to the destination. The choice of direct or indirect delivery depends on the destination address and the address and mask of the host. If the packet cannot be delivered directly, the next-hop router to which the packet is sent may depend on static configuration in the router or on dynamic protocols in which the router participates. If one or more intermediate nodes are in the path between the source and the destination, then in addition to consulting destination addresses and interface addresses and masks, information from dynamic routing protocols may also be consulted.

1.4 Autonomous Systems and the Distinction Between IGPs and EGPs

The Internet is a loose cooperative effort of Internet service providers who voluntarily run the TCP/IP protocol suite as defined by the IETF and other related standards bodies. Examples of the largest ISPs are UUNET, MCI, Sprint, and GTE (formerly BBN). These ISPs are considered large because they have a large backbone infrastructure (a geographically wide topology of fast links) and they correspondingly have a large number of business customers who buy leased lines for dedicated access. Other ISPs are focused on dial-up services and support primarily residential customers. Some examples of large dial-up ISPs are America Online, CompuServe, and Prodigy. In both the dedicated access ISP sector and the dial-up ISP sector, there are many different organizations of varying sizes.

Because the true value of the Internet is its connectedness (anyone connected to the Internet can exchange traffic with anyone else connected to the Internet), these organizations of varying sizes must have a path to reach one another to maintain connectivity. To ensure full connectivity, even in the case of failure, the largest dedicated access ISPs connect directly to one another in many places. Some of the largest dial-up ISPs connect to dedicated access ISPs and other dial-up ISPs in this way, too. Smaller dedicated access ISPs and dial-up ISPs typically pay someone else (such as a larger dedicated access ISP) to provide connectivity for them.

This description shows that the topology of the Internet from an organizational standpoint is quite complicated. This complexity has an effect on the way routing protocols see the network. In the current Internet, one set of protocols is used to run within a certain network infrastructure, whereas a different set of protocols is used between that infrastructure and other parts of the Internet. More specifically, an ISP will run an **IGP** (**internal gateway protocol**) within its backbone to optimize the route taken between points within its network. In addition to the IGP, an ISP will run an **EGP (external gateway protocol)** between its backbone and networks belonging to other ISPs or to customers in order to have full connectivity to the entire Internet. This book uses the terms IGP and EGP, although equivalent terms are Intra-Domain Routing Protocol and Inter-Domain Routing Protocol, respectively.

IGPs and EGPs are general classes of routing protocols and aren't specific routing protocols themselves. This is analogous to the general class of transport protocols, of which TCP and UDP are specific protocols. These two classes of routing protocols have very different purposes. An IGP does what a novice would typically expect from a routing protocol: it figures out how each node in the network gets to every other node in the network in the most optimal way. In this context the word *optimal* refers to the **cost** of the path measured by **metrics** associated with each link in the network. A metric is typically based on delay and so also typically implies something about physical distance. Examples of standard IGPs are **RIP (Routing Information Protocol)**, OSPF (Open Shortest Path First), and IS-IS (Intermediate System to Intermediate System). There are also proprietary IGPs such as Cisco Systems' IGRP and EIGRP.

The area of network infrastructure (primarily routers) over which an IGP runs is typically under the same technical and administrative control, and it defines the boundary of an **AS (autonomous system)**. The concept of an AS is very important to EGPs. Note carefully that an AS is a collection of routers and not a collection of IP prefixes.

The purpose of an EGP is to allow two different ASs to exchange routing information so that data traffic can be forwarded across the AS border. Because an AS border straddles two different areas of technical and administrative control, the specifications and implementations of EGPs include mechanisms for doing **policy routing**, meaning that control can be exerted over which routing information crosses the border between two ASs. (Policy routing is described in detail in a later chapter.) EGPs contain features that are like metrics in IGPs, but unlike IGPs, the function of an EGP is not necessarily to optimize the path that data traffic takes through a backbone. The most relevant EGP to this book is BGP4, the Internet's single de facto EGP. Other, older examples of EGPs are previous versions of BGP as well as GGP (Gateway to Gateway Protocol), Hello, and EGP.[4]

1.5 Distance Vector Versus Link State Routing Protocols

The distinction between IGPs and EGPs is only one dimension along which routing protocols are compared. Another comparison is the basic way in which the routing protocol represents the topology of the network being routed and the IP prefixes reachable via that network. There are two traditional categories into which routing protocols fit: distance vector and link state.

1.5.1 Distance Vector Protocols

Distance vector (DV) protocols are typically understood more easily than link state protocols. Figure 1-7 shows a sample topology that illustrates how DV protocols work. The bold numbers next to the links refer to the cost of the link. Off Router C is connected the prefix **138.39.0.0/16**. For Routers A and B to know to forward packets whose destination addresses start with **138.39**, Router C must first tell Router B that it can reach that network and Router B must then readvertise that information to Router A.

A DV routing protocol running within a particular node starts by

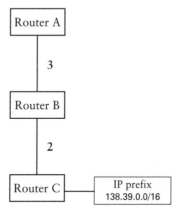

Figure 1-7 *Sample topology for DV*

---

4. The EGP referenced here is a specific protocol called EGP. This is an unfortunate naming conflict, although fortunately the specific protocol EGP is clearly outdated as a general EGP.

initializing a table with information about prefixes to which it is directly connected. The initial state for Router C is shown in Table 1-1. The Cost is zero, and the Heard From column is empty, indicating that the prefix is local.

Table 1-1 Router C at Start-up

Network	Cost	Heard From
138.39.0.0/16	0	*self*

When Router C advertises its routing information to Router B, Router B reacts by adding the information to its table as shown in Table 1-2. The Cost is calculated by adding the metric for the link to the cost of the route that it hears. Note that, for simplicity, this example assumes that only one prefix is being routed.

Table 1-2 Router B after Hearing Router C's Advertisement

Network	Cost	Heard From
138.39.0.0/16	2	Router C

Router B, in turn, advertises its routing information to Router A. The state in Router A is shown in Table 1-3.

Table 1-3 Router A after Hearing Router B's Advertisement

Network	Cost	Heard From
138.39.0.0/16	5	Router B

So at this point Routers A and B can reach destinations inside the 138.39.0.0/16 prefix because of information they receive via a dynamic DV routing protocol, and Router C can reach the prefix because it is directly connected. In other words, the DV routing protocol has done exactly what is needed. By advertising the prefixes to which the nodes are directly connected as well as the routing information they hear from other nodes, all nodes have full connectivity.

The advantage of DV routing protocols is that they are relatively easy to understand and implement. The disadvantages are that they have elements that negatively affect scalability and they cannot handle certain failure situations well. DV routing protocols scale in proportion to the number of prefixes in the network. The reason is that the messages being passed back and forth between neighbors in a DV routing protocol are basically routing tables. Typically, this routing information expires after a certain amount of time so it is necessary to retransmit it at regular intervals. Because modern TCP/IP networks can contain many hundreds or thousands of prefixes, this scaling factor limits the usefulness of DV protocols. As for handling failure, imagine that the line between Routers B and C in Figure 1-7 goes down, as shown in Figure 1-8.

In this case the interface that Router B has toward Router C will go down, so Router B knows that it can no longer reach Router C (and 138.39.0.0/16) through that interface. Router A, however, does not see that Router C is isolated from the network. As a result, Router A continues to advertise the prefix connected to Router C that it heard through Router B. When Router B hears the advertisements for Router C's prefix through Router A, it assumes that it is a legitimate path and further assumes that it can reach Router C's prefix through Router A. When Router B advertises to Router A that Router B's cost to 138.39.0.0/16 is 8 (Router A's 5 plus the link with cost 3 going between Routers A and B), Router A will react by changing its cost for the prefix to 11 because it thinks it reaches the prefix through Router B. This behavior is called **counting to infinity** because the process will continue until the cost for the prefix reaches some maximum value, at which time the prefix is considered unreachable. Fortunately, the specification and implementation of DV routing protocols typically have very low values of infinity (for example, 16) to reduce the length of time it takes to count to infinity. Mechanisms can be added to DV routing protocols to prevent problems such as counting to infinity, but those mechanisms won't be discussed here.

The DV routing protocol most often discussed is the Routing Information Protocol (RIP). RIP is one of the most frequently used routing

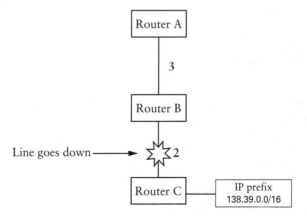

Figure 1-8 *Sample failed topology for DV*

protocols, although its domain of use is limited to small networks with simple topologies.

1.5.2 Link State Protocols

Link state (LS) protocols work very differently from DV protocols. The way that routing information is communicated in an LS routing protocol is through **LSPs** (**link state packet**s).[5] An LSP contains identification information for the router generating it and information about the routers and networks to which it is connected, including the cost to get to those routers and networks.[6] A router generates an LSP for itself and sends it to all its neighbors. A router sends its LSP when it initially comes up, whenever it experiences a topology change (for example, when a link goes down), or periodically to refresh the older LSP in the network. An algorithm runs in the network to ensure that every router's LSP is delivered to every other router in the network. After a given router has received a complete set of LSPs for the network, that router can construct a map of the entire network and then perform computations on the map to decide the shortest path to every destination in the network.

Assuming the topology shown in Figure 1-9, the LSP that each node would generate is shown in Tables 1-4 through 1-7.

Table 1-4 LSP for Router A

Destination	Cost
138.39.0.4/30	—
Router B	4
Router C	1
Router D	10

Table 1-5 LSP for Router B

Destination	Cost
138.39.0.8/30	—
Router A	4
Router C	1

---

5. The term LSP will be used here, although some LS protocols use the term link state advertisement (LSA).
6. This is a simplification. LSPs contain additional information such as a serial number and information about when the LSP should be timed out.

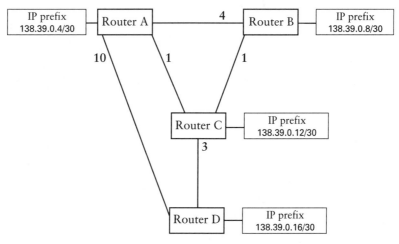

Figure 1-9 *Sample topology for LS*

Table 1-6 LSP for Router C

Destination	Cost
138.39.0.12/30	—
Router A	1
Router B	1
Router D	3

Table 1-7 LSP for Router D

Destination	Cost
138.39.0.16/30	—
Router A	10
Router C	3

After a node generates its LSP, it sends the LSP to all its neighbors—the first stage of the algorithm to distribute the LSP throughout the network. The **flooding algorithm** used is a critical part of an LS protocol. The challenge is to devise an algorithm that has relatively low overhead and distributes the LSP throughout the entire network reasonably fast but doesn't unnecessarily send it to nodes that already have it.

A router will react to certain events (such as the receipt of a new LSP) by taking all the current LSPs that it knows about, called the

LSDB (**link state database**), constructing a map of the network, and calculating the best path to every destination. The process of calculating these best paths is called **running Dijkstra,** for the mathematician who first devised an algorithm for calculating shortest paths in a graph with positively weighted edges. Another name for this process is **running SPF (shortest path first).**

Because the Dijkstra algorithm and the algorithms for doing LSP flooding are somewhat complicated and difficult to describe well in a small amount of space, those descriptions are omitted here. You need not understand these algorithms to have a full understanding of BGP, though, so leaving out the descriptions doesn't reduce the amount of information in this text. Readers who are particularly curious about this topic should see books that focus in detail on protocols such as IS-IS or OSPF. One good reference is Radia Perlman's *Interconnections: Bridges and Routers* (see Appendix A).

One of the important distinctions between LS and DV protocols is that nodes in an LS network have full information about the topology of the network and about all possible paths. One result is that LS protocols typically scale better than DV protocols. The improved scaling can be seen in a couple of ways. First, because LS protocols involve the passing of LSPs and not routing tables, as is done in DV protocols, less information is sent. Second, because LSPs basically reflect the topology of the network, when there is a topology change the amount of new or changed information that must be injected into the network is proportional to the topology change. In DV protocols if there is a topology change, the amount of information circulated is a function of the number of IP prefixes being routed within the network!

The most popular LS protocols are OSPF and IS-IS (both IS-IS per se, which routes only CLNP [Connect-Less Network Protocol], and Integrated IS-IS, which routes both IP and CLNP).

1.6 Classless Inter-Domain Routing

Because IP has been around for almost two decades and, during that time, has seen a tremendous amount of use, its architecture has undergone a number of changes. Originally, it included a concept of *classes* of networks. Although formally this idea of class is no longer present, some parts of the Internet are still **classful**; also, it is difficult to describe what it means to be classless without knowing what it was to be classful.

The Internet is a collection of networks. As a result, IP addresses can be interpreted as having two parts: a part that identifies a network on the Internet and a part that identifies a host on that network. Obviously, not all networks contain the same number of hosts (a dentist office would need to address far fewer hosts than NASA). This was the purpose of classes. There were five classes of networks: Class A, Class B, Class C, Class D, and Class E. Classes D (used for multicast) and E (reserved and currently unused) are not discussed in this book. The difference between Classes A, B, and C is the number of bits used for the network and the number of bits used for the host.

All Class A addresses start with a **0** in the high-order bit; the network part is in the first octet, and the host part is in the following three octets. There are 128 Class A networks, each of which can address approximately 16.7 million hosts. Class A addresses had an implicit mask of **255.0.0.0**.

All Class B addresses start with **10** in the high-order two bits; the network part is in the first two octets, and the host part is in the following two octets. There are 16,384 Class B networks, each of which can address 65,535 hosts. Class B addresses had an implicit mask of **255.255.0.0**.

All Class C addresses start with **110** in the high-order three bits; the network part is in the first three octets, and the host part is in the following octet. There are approximately 2.1 million Class C networks, each of which can address 255 hosts. Class C addresses had an implicit mask of **255.255.255.0**.

A few examples of classful addresses are as follows.

> 18.207.11.121 (**00010010 11001111 00001011 01111001**) is a Class A address in which the network is **18** and the host inside that network is **207.11.121**.

> 128.4.151.3 (**10000000 00000100 10010111 00000011**) is a Class B address in which the network is **128.4** and the host inside that network is **151.3**.

> 198.165.13.100 (**11000110 10100101 00001101 01100100**) is a Class C address in which the network is **198.165.13** and the host inside that network is **100**.

The idea of network classes is no longer formally part of the IP architecture. The Internet standardized on Classless Inter-Domain Routing
(CIDR), a system to improve the scaling factor of routing in the Internet. For CIDR to achieve its goal, addresses must be allocated using a
certain method, and that method is incompatible with the concept of
class. The logical question at this point is why was CIDR done? The
answer is that the Internet was growing faster than the routing infrastructure could support, and something needed to be done to keep the
Internet working. The specific problems CIDR was supposed to solve
were the size and growth rate of the routing tables and the exhaustion
of the IP address space. CIDR most immediately addresses the routing
table problem, but it also has an effect on the lifetime of the address
space.[7]

CIDR got rid of the idea of an implicit mask based on the class of
the network; instead, it requires that explicit masks be passed in inter-
domain routing protocols. This change seems fairly minor, but it has
an important result on routing. Consider Figure 1-10.

Notice that the service provider has a number of customers, all of
them numbered from Class C addresses that start with 204.71; but
despite this relationship, the service provider announces each of the
networks individually into the global Internet routing mesh. With
CIDR, the picture in Figure 1-10 can be improved to look like the configuration in Figure 1-11.

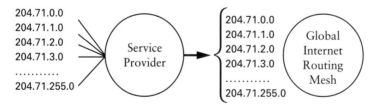

Figure 1-10 *Inter-domain routing without CIDR*

---

7. For historical data about the size of a full Internet routing table and the
effectiveness of CIDR, see http://www.employees.org/~tbates/cidr-report.html.

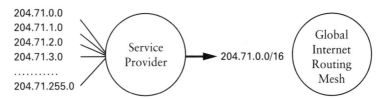

204.71.0.0
204.71.1.0
204.71.2.0
204.71.3.0
....
204.71.255.0

Service Provider

204.71.0.0/16

Global Internet Routing Mesh

Figure 1-11 *Inter-domain routing with CIDR*

With CIDR, the service provider can **aggregate** the classful networks used by its customers into a single classless advertisement; the result is that it can provide routing for hundreds of customers by injecting only one advertisement into the global Internet routing mesh. CIDR summarizes, or abstracts, routing information so that the size of a router's routing table is reduced while its level of connectivity is maintained.

In Figure 1-11 the advertisement is shown as **204.71.0.0/16**. The /16 is the prefix length, a way of expressing the explicit mask that CIDR requires; it is a shortcut for **255.255.0.0** in that the high-order 16 bits are **1** in the mask. As examples, a Class A network would have a prefix length of /8 and a Class C network would have a prefix length of /24. CIDR allows network prefixes to be arbitrary lengths (as opposed to the classful system, in which prefixes had to be an even multiple of an octet); for example, **204.70.2.0/23** is a valid classless network.

In this instance CIDR allows us to reduce the amount of global routing information because of the hierarchical nature of the addressing. In other words, we can aggregate networks and do hierarchical routing because the addressing is hierarchical. For the Internet to make good use of CIDR, the addressing must be done carefully. The easiest way to ensure hierarchical addressing is to have sites connecting to the Internet to obtain addresses from their providers rather than a central repository. Note that in the preceding example the service provider doesn't see any reduction in the size of its routing table for the aggregate; the savings are seen by *other* providers in the Internet. The reason is that although the service provider injects only one advertisement into the Internet, inside its own network it must carry the specific routes so that it can know how to get to each individual customer. The rest of the Internet needs to know only to go to the service provider for anything under 204.71, but the service provider itself needs to know how to get to each individual customer. In other words, the rest of the Internet carries the aggregate while the service provider carries the *more-specifics*.

Because CIDR allows prefixes of arbitrary lengths to be carried in inter-domain routing, it must have a way of handling overlapping prefixes. For example, imagine that a router hears the prefix 138.39.0.0/16 from one neighbor and also hears 138.39.16.0/24 from another neighbor. CIDR formalizes the idea of **longest match**, which says that a router must forward a packet based on the most specific forwarding entry that the router has for the packet's destination address. In this example, if a router receives a packet destined for 138.39.16.32, the router will use the 138.39.16.0/24 forwarding entry because it matches the destination address more specifically than the /16 forwarding entry. On the other hand, a packet destined for 138.39.82.45 will be forwarded based on the /16 forwarding entry because, in this case, the /16 is the longest match.

CIDR helped ease the Internet's problems in two ways. First, because CIDR let ISPs aggregate routes, after initial deployment of CIDR the size of the Internet routing table went down in absolute numbers. What's more, the rate of growth was slowed. For now, CIDR keeps the demand of Internet routing within the reach of current-generation commercial routers. Next, by allowing networks to be assigned on arbitrary bit boundaries, CIDR extended the lifetime of the address space as a whole. Before CIDR, if an organization needed enough address space to number 500 hosts, a single Class C would not have been enough, so an entire Class B would have to be allocated. This was overkill and resulted in the address space being poorly utilized. In this situation, using CIDR, the organization could be assigned a 23-bit prefix (that is, two Class Cs).

CIDR is critical to the functioning of the Internet. If BGP4, which was created primarily to support CIDR, had not been deployed, the ability of the Internet to grow would be severely constrained. It is also true, however, that CIDR is simply a tool. For CIDR to make a difference, address registries must base address assignment on the CIDR strategies, and network operators must configure BGP in their routers so that the aggregation made possible by the addressing actually happens.

Sometimes there are complications to the achievement of aggregation. From a pragmatic standpoint, configuring BGP with CIDR aggregation requires a relatively intimate understanding of IP addressing—a skill that is not widely available. In this same vein, the ability to plan a network and its associated configuration processes to accommodate aggregation even in the face of extreme growth is not a trivial task. Aside from these issues—for which there are clear answers—there are other issues that do not have a single, clear answer. Two examples of these thornier issues are **multihoming** and **proxy aggregation**. In multihoming, an Internet subscriber procures more than one link to the Internet for the sake of reliability or performance. (Multihoming is considered in more detail in a future section.) Proxy aggregation is a type of aggregation in which the AS that has the aggregatable address space depends on another AS to perform the aggregation.

1.7 Setting the Tone for Understanding BGP

Starting with Chapter 2, many specifics of BGP will be discussed. Before we get into that, however, it seems helpful to give a high-level view of what BGP does and the framework in which it accomplishes its function.

Using terms explained and developed earlier in this chapter, BGP can be described as an EGP based on DV algorithms that uses TCP as its transport protocol. Because of assumptions of BGP and, indeed, because of its use of TCP, BGP is a protocol that happens between exactly two nodes. At any given time, a network may have many BGP sessions occurring within it, and a router may be participating in many BGP sessions; but the important point is that for an individual BGP session, only two routers are involved. Two routers that exchange routing information dynamically with BGP establish a TCP connection between themselves and then pass BGP messages over that connection. The messages they pass include ones to open the BGP session, to inform the neighbor about new routes that are active, to inform the neighbor of old routes that are no longer active, to inform the neighbor that the connection is still viable, and to report unusual conditions before terminating the TCP connection. When a router advertises a prefix to one of its BGP neighbors, that information is considered valid until the first router explicitly advertises that the information is no longer valid or until the BGP session itself is lost. In other words, BGP does not require that routing information be refreshed.

A fundamental principle of BGP is that when BGP speaker A advertises to its neighbor B that it has a path for reaching a particular IP prefix, B can be certain that A is actively using that path to reach the destination. The observant reader will note that this behavior fits DV routing protocols well.

Another feature of BGP is that when a BGP speaker advertises a prefix to one of its BGP neighbors, a number of **attributes** are associated with that prefix. Attributes are used heavily in BGP to carry a wide range of information. Examples of uses for attributes are as follows:

- Next hops where packets destined for the prefix should be sent
- Various kinds of metrics specifying degrees of preference for the route
- The path of ASs that the routing announcement has traversed
- The way that the prefix entered the routing table at the source AS

New attributes have been added to BGP over time in order to add features. This extensibility has been instrumental in allowing BGP to accommodate the Internet's growth and the changing demands made of BGP.

2

The BGP Protocol

Chapter 1 provides an introduction to IP and presents a brief framework for BGP. This chapter goes into a low level of detail about BGP in terms of the protocol machinery, message formats, route advertisement, route withdrawal, route selection, and so on.

2.1 Bringing Up a BGP Session

When two routers are configured to speak BGP with each other for the sake of exchanging dynamic routing information, the first step is to establish a connection between them. The two endpoints are called **BGP peers** of each other, and together they form a **BGP session**. For both ends of the BGP session to be sure that none of the information one has sent to the other has been lost, the connection established between the routers must be reliable. There are two ways to achieve this reliability requirement. The first is for BGP to invent a protocol internal to itself that accomplishes the orderly delivery of messages, detects duplicates, recognizes when information has been lost and retransmits it, controls the rate of sending so that the receiving end isn't overloaded, and so on. The other option is for BGP to use an existing protocol that does exactly these things. BGP takes the latter approach, specifically using TCP. Before an attempt has been made to establish a TCP connection between the two endpoints, the BGP session is said to be in the *Idle* state.

When one of the endpoints starts an attempt to establish a TCP connection, the BGP session on that endpoint is said to be in the *Connect* state. If a TCP connection cannot be established after a certain amount of time, the endpoint transitions to the *Active* state, in which it periodically retries to establish a connection. After the TCP connection has been established, the endpoints can be assured that, as long as there is a viable connection between them, messages will be delivered reliably. Furthermore, the endpoints know that if the connection ceases to be viable, they will be told about it locally by TCP. This arrangement allows the BGP messages themselves to be very simple and include only the necessary information with minimal overhead. One feature BGP must contain and cannot rely on TCP to support is a **keepalive**. In a general sense, a keepalive is a signal from endpoint A to endpoint B that A is still up and running. Keepalives are often used on circuits connecting routers as a way of identifying failed circuits. TCP itself does not include a keepalive, so BGP must account for that lack.

After the TCP connection has been established, the two ends of the connection send messages to each other that are formatted in the way mandated by the BGP protocol. One endpoint's reaction to a message from the other can be an explicit BGP message in response. Or it could be a change to an entry in routing or forwarding tables, or there could be no reaction at all.

At a high level, the first thing that BGP neighbors do when the TCP connection is established is to identify themselves in a number of ways to each other. When an endpoint sends this identification message, it transitions to the *OpenSent* state. When an endpoint receives a similar identification message from its neighbor, it transitions to the *Open-Confirm* state. Based on this identification information, each neighbor has the right to accept or refuse the connection. If the connection is refused, typically an error notification of some kind is made and the TCP connection is closed. If the connection is accepted, each side sends an explicit notification that it is accepting the connection. When an endpoint receives this acceptance, it transitions to the *Established* state.

At this point, the BGP session is considered fully active, and for the first time routes can be exchanged. At this point it is necessary for each end to advertise a route for every prefix that it wants the other end to know. In other words, if Router A has 50,000 prefixes and it is configured to send all of them to Router B, a large number of messages will be sent advertising all these prefixes. After these initial messages have been exchanged, though, Router A needs to inform Router B only of changes; the protocol does not require that Router A refresh information about any of these prefixes to Router B. One important feature of BGP is its support for policy, meaning that a BGP speaker does not have to accept every route that it learns from a neighbor. Instead, a BGP speaker can selectively accept and reject routes based on configuration.

BGP sessions typically stay in the Established state most of the time. If an error occurs while a given BGP session is active, the neighbor perceiving the error sends a message to its neighbor identifying the error and then closes the TCP connection, thus transitioning back to the *Idle* state. After the TCP connection is broken, each end must stop using routing information that it heard from the other. If the connection between BGP neighbors is broken (for example, because one of the routers goes down or there is no longer a viable path between them), the TCP connection times out and each end stops using the routing information it heard from the other.

2.2 The BGP Message Types

This section describes in great detail the types and formats of messages that are sent between BGP speakers on the TCP connection.

2.2.1 Common Header

A **common header** precedes all BGP messages. The format of the common header is shown in Figure 2-1.

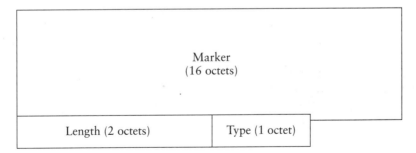

Figure 2-1 *Common header*

The Marker field can be used for two different purposes: synchronization and security. The value of this field depends on the message being sent and the type of security used, if any. If the message being sent is an OPEN message, implying that this is the first message being sent between peers, the Marker field contains all 1s. If, when the BGP session was established, a security option was specified, the Marker field is predictable based on that security option. If no security option is used, the Marker field is all 1s for all message types.

The Length field specifies the length of the entire BGP message, including the common header.

The Type field specifies the BGP message being sent. The possible values are

- OPEN (1)
- UPDATE (2)
- NOTIFICATION (3)
- KEEPALIVE (4)

Following the common header are zero or more additional octets for the particular BGP message being sent. The additional octets, if any, are interpreted according to the Type field in the common header. The four message types are described in the next four sections.

2.2.2 OPEN

An OPEN message is the first message sent after the TCP connection is established. The purpose of the OPEN message is for each endpoint to identify itself to the other and to agree on protocol parameters, such as timers. The format of an OPEN message is shown in Figure 2-2.

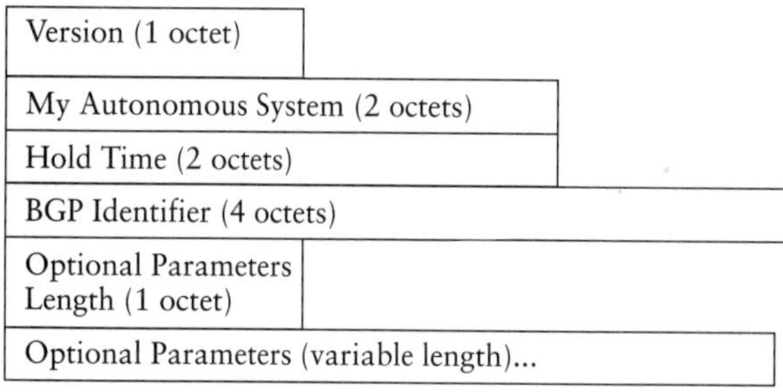

```
┌─────────────────────────┐
│ Version (1 octet)       │
├─────────────────────────────────────┐
│ My Autonomous System (2 octets)     │
├─────────────────────────────────────┤
│ Hold Time (2 octets)                │
├────────────────────────────────────────────────┐
│ BGP Identifier (4 octets)                       │
├─────────────────────────┐
│ Optional Parameters     │
│ Length (1 octet)        │
├──────────────────────────────────────────┐
│ Optional Parameters (variable length)... │
└──────────────────────────────────────────┘
```

Figure 2-2 *OPEN message*

The Version field specifies the BGP version that the sender of the OPEN message is using. The presence of this field gives two BGP speakers a crude negotiation mechanism for using the highest common version number. For example, if a BGP4 speaker sends an OPEN message to a BGP3 speaker, the BGP3 speaker returns an error message specifying that it doesn't support version 4 and then closes the TCP connection. The BGP4 speaker can react to this error message by opening a new TCP connection and behaving according to the BGP3 specification, thus being compatible.

The My Autonomous System field specifies the **ASN** (**autonomous system number**) of the router sending the OPEN message. As discussed earlier, the Internet is a collection of routing domains. Each of these routing domains is uniquely identified by an ASN. BGP speakers are configured with their ASN and the ASNs of each BGP neighbor. When an OPEN message is received from a neighbor and processed, the My Autonomous System field is compared to the ASN configured for that neighbor. If the values match, processing continues. Otherwise, an error message is sent and the TCP connection is closed.

The Hold Time field specifies the number of seconds that the sender of the OPEN message proposes to use as a **hold timer**. The hold timer is the maximum length of time that one endpoint will wait to hear something from the other endpoint (either an UPDATE message or a KEEPALIVE) before assuming that the BGP session is down. A Hold Time field with a value of zero means that the sender is proposing not to exchange KEEPALIVE messages. (This mode of operation is discouraged because it might result in one of the BGP speakers not knowing that the other one went down.) A nonzero Hold Time must be at least three seconds. The hold timer chosen for the BGP session is the minimum of the value configured locally and the value advertised by the neighbor. The protocol explicitly allows neighbors to reject an OPEN message if the value of the Hold Time field is unacceptable.

The BGP Identifier field contains a value used to identify the BGP speaker. When a given BGP speaker sends an OPEN message, that BGP speaker chooses the value to put into the BGP Identifier field. The identifier must be unique, but it isn't required to have any particular addressing semantics. For convenience, though, the identifier is typically one of the IP addresses assigned to the router. The address chosen often is not one associated with a physical interface but with a distinguished virtual interface. A given BGP speaker uses the same BGP identifier for every BGP session.

The Optional Parameters Length field specifies the length of any options included in the OPEN message. If no options are present, the value of this field is zero.

The Optional Parameters field contains any optional parameters included in the OPEN message. Optional parameters are encoded as a one-octet parameter type, one-octet parameter length, and variable-length parameter value.

The base specification for BGP4 specifies a single optional parameter: authentication information. This optional parameter is parameter type 1 and is encoded as a one-octet authentication code followed by variable-length authentication data. The authentication code identifies the authentication mechanism being used. The specification for an authentication mechanism must contain the authentication code, the way to interpret the authentication data, and the computation to send and receive the Marker field in the common header.

Having said all this about the authentication information optional parameter, it should be noted that the base BGP4 specification does not define any authentication codes. The reasons for this, along with a different mechanism for securing BGP sessions, are described in Section 4.4 of Chapter 4.

One other optional parameter has been added to BGP4 for capability negotiation. This optional parameter is described later in the book.

2.2.3 UPDATE

The UPDATE message is the primary message used to communicate information between two BGP speakers. When a BGP speaker advertises a prefix to a BGP neighbor or withdraws a previously advertised prefix, that BGP speaker uses an UPDATE message. The format of an UPDATE message is shown in Figure 2-3.

The Withdrawn Routes Length field indicates the length of the Withdrawn Routes field in octets. The specification calls this field Unfeasible Routes Length, but we prefer the term *withdrawn* to *unfeasible* because it is more consistent with other language used.

The Withdrawn Routes field contains a list of IP prefixes for which the sender of the UPDATE message no longer wishes to forward packets.

When Router A sends an UPDATE to Router B with a withdrawal for a prefix, it typically means that the path between Router A and the prefix is at least temporarily not viable. Router A may not know about the prefix directly and instead may have heard about the prefix through a BGP neighbor or a neighbor of some other dynamic routing protocol. The main point here is that Router A must withdraw the prefix to Router B or else Router B will continue to send packets destined for the prefix to Router A. IP prefixes are represented in Figure 2-4. The Length field in the representation of an IP prefix indicates the number of **bits** in the prefix. In other words, this is the prefix length or network mask.

The Prefix field in the representation of an IP prefix contains the prefix itself followed by enough bits to make the length of the whole field an integer multiple of 8 bits. The purpose of this padding is simply to make the field be some number of whole octets because the protocol messages are parsed as a stream of octets and not a stream of individual bits. On receipt of an IP prefix, the value of the trailing bits must be ignored.

Returning to the UPDATE message, the Total Path Attributes Length field indicates the length of the Path Attributes field.

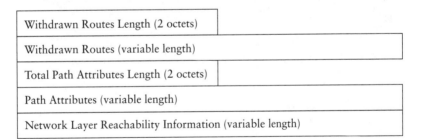

Withdrawn Routes Length (2 octets)
Withdrawn Routes (variable length)
Total Path Attributes Length (2 octets)
Path Attributes (variable length)
Network Layer Reachability Information (variable length)

Figure 2-3 *UPDATE message*

Length (1 octet)
Prefix (variable length)

Figure 2-4 *IP prefix*

The Path Attributes field contains a list of BGP attributes associated with the prefixes in the Network Layer Reachability Information field. BGP's attributes are one of its most important features. Attributes describe the prefixes in ways such as how the prefix came to be routed by BGP, the path of ASs through which the prefix has been advertised until this point, and metrics expressing degrees of preference for this prefix. Except for the prefixes themselves, it is the attributes that carry the important information. The exact attributes exchanged and the values of those attributes can control which prefixes are exchanged via BGP sessions, which one of multiple paths for a particular prefix is used, and so on. The base specification for BGP4 includes a number of attributes, although additional attributes have been added over time and are commonly seen in the Internet.

Because these attributes are important, they are described later in a dedicated section. This section describes how attributes are formatted syntactically and explains the semantic meaning of the control bits in the attribute encoding. As shown in Figure 2-5, each attribute is encoded as an attribute type, attribute length, and attribute value.

The Attribute Type field is a two-octet field, as shown in Figure 2-6. The Attribute Flags field is a bit string containing four binary values describing the attribute and four unused bits. From high-order to low-order (starting from the left in the diagram), the meanings of the bits are as follows.

   1. The first bit is called the Optional bit. If this bit is set (1), the attribute is *optional*. If this bit is clear (0), the attribute is

| Attribute Type (2 octets) |
| Attribute Length (1 or 2 octets) |
| Attribute Value (variable length) |

Figure 2-5 *Attribute encoding*

| Attribute Flags (1 octet) | Attribute Type Code (1 octet) |

Figure 2-6 *Attribute type field*

well-known. A **well-known attribute** must be recognized by all BGP implementations and, if appropriate, passed to BGP peers. An optional attribute, on the other hand, is not required to be present in all BGP implementations.

2. The second bit is the Transitive bit. For well-known attributes, this bit must be set (**1**). For optional attributes, this bit controls whether the attribute is passed to other BGP peers (it is **transitive**) or not (it is **nontransitive**). If the bit is set (**1**), the attribute is passed on. If the bit is clear (**0**), the attribute is not passed on.

3. The third bit is the Partial bit. It indicates whether BGP implementations in the path between the source of a prefix's announcement and a receiver of that prefix understand an optional transitive attribute. For example, imagine that an optional attribute requires information to be added to the attribute as the prefix announcement makes its way through the network. An example of the use for such an attribute would be to record the routers through which the announcement passes. The problem is that, if the attribute is optional, it is possible that not all of the routers support it. On receipt of an optional transitive attribute it would be helpful to know whether any information has been lost along the way because one or more routers didn't implement the option. So if Router A hears a prefix from Router B that contains an optional transitive attribute not included in Router A's implementation. If Router A passes that prefix to Router C, it must set (**1**) the Partial bit. For well-known attributes and optional nontransitive attributes, this bit must be clear (**0**).

4. The fourth bit is the Extended Length bit. If this bit is clear (**0**), it indicates that the length of the attribute is represented in one octet. If this bit is set (**1**), it indicates that the length of the attribute is represented in two octets. This bit may be set only if the length of the attribute is truly greater than 255 octets.

The attribute type code is a number assigned by the IANA (Internet Assigned Numbers Authority) that uniquely identifies the attribute from all others. The base BGP specification includes the attribute types for all the attributes it defines. When a new attribute is defined, its specification must include the attribute type for identification.

The Attribute Length field is one or two octets long, depending on the value of the Extended Length bit in the Attribute Flags field. It indicates the length of the Attribute Value field.

The Attribute Value field contains the actual value of the attribute and is parsed and processed according to the Attribute Flags and Attribute Type fields.

Returning again to the UPDATE message, the NLRI (Network Layer Reachability Information) field contains a list of prefixes, each of which is formatted as shown earlier in Figure 2-4. The number of prefixes in the list is limited only by the size of the packet that can be sent between the BGP speakers. It is important to understand that every attribute in the Path Attributes field applies to every prefix in the NLRI field. This means that if a BGP speaker wants to advertise multiple prefixes in a single UPDATE message, the speaker must advertise only prefixes that share all attributes. Note further that because of the overhead of processing an individual message, regardless of that message's length, BGP implementers are encouraged to support the sending of multiple prefixes in a single UPDATE message. The result is that BGP implementations should support the ability to quickly find prefixes that have attributes in common.

2.2.4 NOTIFICATION

If an error occurs during the life of a BGP session, the NOTIFICATION message type (see Figure 2-7) can be used to signal the presence of such an error before the underlying TCP connection is closed. This arrangement allows the administrator of the remote system to receive an indication of why the BGP session was terminated. Note that the BGP specification requires that the TCP connection be closed immediately after sending a NOTIFICATION.

The Error Code field identifies the type of error that was encountered. Possible types of errors and their error codes are as follows.

- Message Header Error (1) indicates an error in processing a common header or the message in general.
- OPEN Message Error (2) indicates an error in processing an OPEN message.

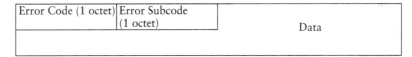

Figure 2-7 *NOTIFICATION message*

- UPDATE Message Error (3) indicates an error in processing an UPDATE message.
- Hold Timer Expired (4) indicates that more time has passed since the receipt of a message (OPEN, UPDATE, or KEEPALIVE) than is allowed by the negotiated hold timer.
- Finite State Machine Error (5) indicates that an illegal event was received for the current state.
- Cease (6) is the error code used when no other error code applies but the BGP speaker chooses to terminate the BGP session.

The Error Subcode field gives more-specific information about the error encountered.

For message header errors, the supported subcodes are as follows.

- Connection Not Synchronized (1) indicates that the Marker field was not predicted correctly.
- Bad Message Length (2) indicates that the message length was either less than the minimum allowed by the protocol syntax or more than the maximum allowed on the link.
- Bad Message Type (3) indicates that the message type was not OPEN, UPDATE, NOTIFICATION, or KEEPALIVE.

For OPEN message header errors, the following subcodes are supported.

- Unsupported Version Number (1) indicates that the sender of the NOTIFICATION does not support the BGP version specified by the sender of the OPEN message.
- Bad Peer AS (2) indicates that the My Autonomous System field in the OPEN message does not match the configuration of the peer in the system that sent the NOTIFICATION message.
- Bad BGP Identifier (3) indicates that the BGP Identifier field in the OPEN message does not match the configuration of the peer in the system that sent the NOTIFICATION message.

- Unsupported Optional Parameter (4) indicates that the sender of the NOTIFICATION message does not support an optional parameter included in the OPEN message.
- Authentication Failure (5) indicates that the sender of the NOTIFICATION message could not authenticate the peer that sent the OPEN message.
- Unacceptable Hold Time (6) indicates that the sender of the NOTIFICATION message is rejecting the BGP session based on the Hold Timer field in the OPEN message.

For UPDATE message errors, supported subcodes are as follows.

- Malformed Attribute List (1) indicates that the sender of the NOTIFICATION encountered an error while parsing the Path Attributes field in the UPDATE message.
- Unrecognized Well-known Attribute (2) indicates that the sender of the NOTIFICATION message does not support an attribute received in an UPDATE message whose Attribute Flags field indicates that the attribute is well-known.
- Missing Well-known Attribute (3) indicates that, when processing an UPDATE message, the sender of the NOTIFICATION message did not correctly receive all required attributes.
- Attribute Flags Error (4) indicates that the Attribute Flags field of an attribute in the Path Attributes field did not make sense.
- Attribute Length Error (5) indicates that the length of an attribute in the UPDATE message is syntactically incorrect (for example, the length of the attribute is longer than the remainder of the message).
- Invalid ORIGIN Attribute (6) indicates that the value specified for the ORIGIN attribute is not one of the three allowed values.
- AS Routing Loop (7) indicates that the sender of the NOTIFICATION received an UPDATE message containing a looping prefix.
- Invalid NEXT-HOP Attribute (8) indicates that the value of the NEXT-HOP attribute in the UPDATE message is invalid.
- Optional Attribute Error (9) indicates that an error was encountered when processing an optional attribute included in the UPDATE message.
- Invalid Network Field (10) indicates that an error was encountered when processing a prefix in the UPDATE message.

- Malformed AS-PATH (11) indicates that an error was encountered when processing the AS-PATH attribute in the UPDATE message.

The Data field may be present depending on the error code and error subcode. Particular error conditions can be specified to include data in the Data field so that an indication about which part of the message it considers to be in error can be sent to the remote end.

2.2.5 KEEPALIVE

BGP neighbors send a KEEPALIVE message to each other to confirm that the connection between them is still active. The rate at which KEEPALIVEs are sent depends on the hold timer negotiated and the frequency at which UPDATE messages are sent. The protocol requires that some data be sent between neighbors before the hold timer expires, although this data can be either a KEEPALIVE or an UPDATE message if there is actual routing information to send. If an UPDATE message is sent, the hold timer is reinitialized to the negotiated value. Syntactically, a KEEPALIVE message is simply a common header with no other data.

2.3 Conceptual Model of Operation

The BGP4 specification uses a specific set of terms to discuss the way a BGP implementation should behave with respect to learning a prefix on one BGP session and then possibly readvertising that prefix to other BGP neighbors. The point is not to dictate a particular way that BGP should be implemented; an implementer can take any desired approach. Instead, the point is to describe the conceptual way that a BGP implementation learns about prefixes from neighbors, how the implementation uses the prefixes locally, and how the implementation informs other neighbors about the prefixes.

The specification introduces the terms **Adj-RIB-In, Loc-RIB**, and **Adj-RIB-Out**. The **RIB** in each of these terms refers to a routing information base, which is simply another name for a routing table. An Adj-RIB-In is the place where prefixes learned from a particular neighbor are stored. There are as many Adj-RIBs-In as there are peers. Because a BGP speaker can learn about the same prefix through multiple BGP neighbors, there must be a process to analyze all the prefixes in all the Adj-RIBs-In and decide which candidate paths to the prefixes to use. The prefixes that are selected for use are stored in the Loc-RIB, and there is only one Loc-RIB per system. Finally, the Adj-RIBs-Out are used to store prefixes to be advertised to a particular neighbor. As with the Adj-RIBs-In, there is one Adj-RIB-Out for each peer.

2.4 Base Standard Path Attributes

Attributes are one of BGP's most important features. Attributes express most of the information describing the routed prefixes. The way that attributes are encoded allows BGP to be extended with new features over time without the need to change the base protocol. This section describes the attributes defined in the original BGP specification. In addition to describing the purpose and syntax of each attribute, the values of the attribute flags of the field are also included. Additional attributes added to BGP are described in a later chapter.

2.4.1 ORIGIN

This attribute describes how a prefix came to be routed by BGP at the origin AS. Understanding this requires understanding how routing is configured in a practical sense. Prefixes don't magically appear in routing protocols, but instead they are learned from some other source and are then *injected* into BGP. Prefixes are learned from directly connected interfaces, from manually configured static routes, through dynamic internal routing protocols, or through dynamic external routing protocols. The administrator of a router can configure it to take prefixes learned from such sources and route them through BGP. Possible values for the ORIGIN attribute are IGP, EGP, or INCOMPLETE.

The ORIGIN attribute's type code is 1, and it is a well-known mandatory attribute. The length of the field is always one octet, and the allowed values are as follows.

- IGP (1) indicates that the prefix was learned from an IGP.
- EGP (2) indicates that the prefix was learned through the EGP protocol.

- INCOMPLETE (3) indicates that the prefix was learned through something other than an IGP or the EGP protocol. In practice, this is most often seen for static routes.

2.4.2 AS-PATH

This attribute contains the ASs through which the announcement for the prefix has passed. As a prefix is passed between ASs, each AS adds its ASN to the AS-PATH attribute. In other words, the AS-PATH is appended to as the prefix is distributed through the Internet. Consider the picture shown in Figure 2-8.

In this example, the prefix **138.39.0.0/16** is routed by AS1. Through some mechanism, the prefix is injected into BGP within AS1 and then advertised to AS2. As AS1 advertises the prefix to AS2, it makes sure that AS1 appears in the AS-PATH attribute. In this way, AS2 can see that AS1 was the first AS to inject the prefix into BGP; in this context AS1 is called the *origin AS*. Assuming that AS2 chooses to pass the prefix to AS3, AS2 appends its ASN to the AS-PATH. So at this point AS3 has full visibility into the fact that the prefix originated in AS1 and was then passed to AS2 and from there into AS3. This, by itself, is useful for the operators of the ASs. However, it also provides the critical feature of detecting and preventing looping announcements. Specifically, if AS3 chooses to pass the announcement for **138.39.0.0/16** to AS1, when AS1 receives that announcement it can decide not to accept it because it actually originated in AS1 and it is therefore unlikely that AS3 could have a better path to that route.

This description of looping routing announcements is true in virtually all practical situations. In theory, however, there are times when

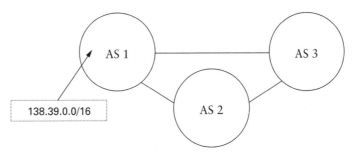

Figure 2-8 *Example topology for AS-PATH*

it would be useful to allow what might seem like a looping routing announcement. Consider Figure 2-9. This situation is the same as Figure 2-8 except that here AS1 has become partitioned into two disjointed areas: (a) and (b). The prefix **138.39.0.0/16** is reachable within the AS by partition (a) but not by partition (b). In this case, it might be helpful if the prefix announcement could go from partition (a) to AS2 to AS3 and then back to AS1 into partition (b). This could be called *partition healing* with BGP. Some BGP implementations support configuration to accept prefixes with the local ASN in the AS-PATH, but others don't support it. Even those implementations that support the configuration option typically don't actually use it.

The AS-PATH attribute is type code 2 and is a well-known mandatory attribute. It is encoded as a sequence of AS-PATH segments. Each of these segments is encoded as a path segment type, path segment length, and path segment value. The Path Segment Type field is a one-octet field with two allowable values.

- AS-SET (1) contains an unordered set of ASNs.
- AS-SEQUENCE (2) contains an ordered set of ASNs.

In practice, almost all routes advertised in BGP have a single AS-SEQUENCE in the AS-PATH attribute. The purpose of AS-SETs is to support aggregation of routes with different AS-PATHs. Specifically, imagine that a router has a route for **138.39.0/17** with an AS-PATH of "100 200 15" and a route for **138.39.128/17** with an AS-PATH of "47 200 15," and it needs to create an aggregate for **138.39/16**. Because the

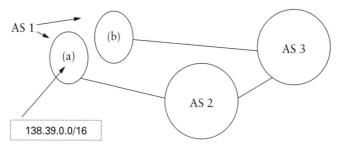

Figure 2-9 *Example partitioned topology*

AS-PATHs are different, the aggregate created by the router will have an AS-PATH attribute of "{100, 47} 200 15." The "{100, 47}" is encoded as an AS-SET, and the "200 15" is encoded as an AS-SEQUENCE. The reason AS-SEQUENCEs are rare is that most aggregation is done on more-specifics that have identical AS-PATH attributes.

The path segment type(s) associated with a prefix depends on what has happened to that prefix with respect to aggregation. The exact uses of the two different path segment types are described later. The Path Segment Length field is a one-octet field indicating the number of ASs in the segment. Finally, the path segment value is a list of ASNs, each of which is two octets long. Note that the length of the path segment value is actually twice that of the path segment length because the path segment length indicates the number of ASs and not the number of octets.

2.4.3 NEXT-HOP

When BGP speaker A advertises a prefix to BGP speaker B, A includes the address of the *next hop* node, which is the node to send data packets to in order to get the packets closer to the destination. The NEXT-HOP attribute is used for this purpose. Often the NEXT-HOP address is the same as the BGP speaker that sends the UPDATE message, but at other times the addresses are different. Consider Figure 2-10.

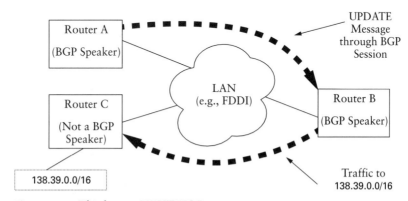

Figure 2-10 *Third-party NEXT-HOP*

This diagram shows routers A, B, and C directly connected with one another over a LAN such as FDDI. A and B are BGP speakers and have a BGP session with each other, whereas C does not support BGP. This diagram shows A sending an UPDATE message to B for 138.39.0.0/16 and including a NEXT-HOP attribute with C's address. The result is that when B receives a packet destined for a host within the 138.39.0.0/16 prefix, B sends those packets directly to C even though C does not directly speak BGP. This feature of the protocol, called **third-party next hop**, typically requires special configuration on A and assumes that B accepts third-party next hops. This feature can be useful when several routers are on a LAN but only some of them support BGP.

The NEXT-HOP attribute is type code 3 and is a well-known mandatory attribute. The attribute is encoded by placing the 32 bits (four octets) of the IP address directly after the Type Code field.

2.4.4 MULTI-EXIT-DISCRIMINATOR

If two ASs connect to each other in more than one place, it is useful to be able to choose the optimal link to reach a particular prefix in or behind that AS. The MULTI-EXIT-DISCRIMINATOR attribute (also commonly abbreviated MED) can be used to carry a metric expressing a degree of preference. Consider Figure 2-11.

In this diagram AS1 and AS2 are connected to each other in two places over Links A and B. In addition to representing a physical circuit, each link represents a BGP session. We also see that AS3

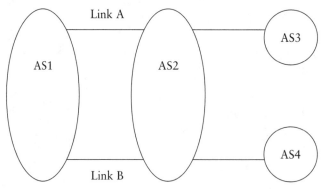

Figure 2-11 *Example topology for MULTI-EXIT-DISCRIMINATOR*

connects to AS2 in a location close to Link A, and that AS4 connects to AS2 in a location close to Link B. AS2 can include MULTI-EXIT-DISCRIMINATORs in the prefixes that it sends to AS1 on each of the peering sessions as a way of expressing how close the prefix is to the endpoint inside AS2. AS1 can then use those attributes to decide which link to AS2 is optimal for which destinations. For example, imagine a prefix internal to AS2 that is close to Link A. When AS2 advertises that prefix to AS1 over the BGP session on Link A, a MULTI-EXIT-DISCRIMINATOR value of 10 can be used, but when AS2 advertises that same prefix to AS1 over the BGP session on Link B, a value of 50 can be used. From these two values AS1 can decide that Link A is the optimal link to use when sending to that prefix. Note that AS2 does, in fact, advertise the prefix over both of the BGP sessions so that if one of the links goes down, AS1 still has full connectivity to the prefixes in and behind AS2. Note also that MULTI-EXIT-DISCRIMINATORs can be used by AS2 for prefixes both inside and outside AS2. For example, the MULTI-EXIT-DISCRIMINATOR can be used to instruct AS1 to use Link A when sending traffic to prefixes in AS3 and similarly to instruct AS1 to use Link B when sending traffic to prefixes in AS4.

One important characteristic to note about the MULTI-EXIT-DISCRIMINATOR is that one AS sets the value and a different AS uses that value in deciding which path to choose. For this reason, the MULTI-EXIT-DISCRIMINATOR is typically used only in a provider/ subscriber situation in which one party is being paid by the other to provide service. Assume that ISP1 and ISP2 connect to each other in New York and San Francisco so that ISP1 and ISP2's customers can exchange traffic. In this case the MULTI-EXIT-DISCRIMINATOR could be used so that one of the ISPs has a larger burden for carrying traffic. For example, ISP1 could configure itself to ignore MULTI-EXIT-DISCRIMINATORs received from ISP2 and also could configure itself to send MULTI-EXIT-DISCRIMINATORs to ISP2. In this case, if a customer of ISP1 in San Francisco wanted to exchange traffic with a customer of ISP2 in New York, ISP1 would give the traffic directly to ISP2 in San Francisco and ISP2 would be responsible for carrying the traffic across the country. On the return path, ISP2 would use the MULTI-EXIT-DISCRIMINATORs that ISP1 sent, and it would decide to first send the traffic across the country on its own network and only then to send the traffic to ISP1. Because much of the cost of running an ISP is bandwidth, this kind of practice is inherently unfair without some kind of settlement scheme. For this reason, ISPs typically ignore MULTI-EXIT-DISCRIMINATORs from other ISPs that aren't customers.

The MULTI-EXIT-DISCRIMINATOR attribute is type code 4 and is an optional nontransitive attribute. The length of the attribute is always four octets, and the encoding is an unsigned integer. It is important to note that the attribute is nontransitive.

Consider Figure 2-11 again. If AS1 were to send MULTI-EXIT-DISCRIMINATORs to AS2, AS2 would not pass the MULTI-EXIT-DISCRIMINATORs to AS3 or AS4 because the attribute is nontransitive. This makes sense for a number of reasons. The primary reason is that the values of the attributes are relative to the two links between AS1 and AS2 and have no relevance to other places in the topology. Furthermore, because AS3 and AS4 each has only one link to AS2, there is no need to have any kind of a metric to compare different paths for prefixes because there will always be only one path—for example, for AS3 to reach AS2. It is also important to note that it doesn't always make sense to compare MULTI-EXIT-DISCRIMINATORs between two routes. Imagine, for example, that AS1 learns about two ways to reach 138.39/16: one from AS2 and the other from AS3. In this case it doesn't make sense to compare MULTI-EXIT-DISCRIMINATOR values because the two routes weren't learned from the same AS.

2.4.5 LOCAL-PREF

Because an AS can have many points from which it can leave the AS and enter other areas of the Internet, the AS can potentially know about many paths for reaching the same destination. In Section 2.4.4 we saw a metric that BGP uses for selecting between multiple paths to a prefix when those multiple paths arise from multiple connections between the same ASs. The MULTI-EXIT-DISCRIMINATOR attribute is not sufficient to address the issue of selecting among multiple paths for two reasons. First is the fundamental problem with MULTI-EXIT-DISCRIMINATORs that one AS can dictate the path taken by the other AS, and that is sometimes problematic as described earlier. The second reason is that MULTI-EXIT-DISCRIMINATORs help for choosing among multiple paths only in the case of multiple links between a single pair of ASs; in practice, there are many possible ways for an AS to have multiple paths for the same prefix. The LOCAL-PREF attribute is a metric used to select among multiple paths to the same prefix, and it does not have the limitations and disadvantages of the MULTI-EXIT-DISCRIMINATOR. Consider Figure 2-12.

In this example AS1 is connected to AS2 and AS3. AS2 and AS3 each has its own connection to AS4. There is a BGP session running on each of these links. AS1 originates the prefix **138.39.0.0/16** into BGP and advertises the prefix to AS2 and AS3. After AS2 and AS3 have the prefix, each of them can pass it to AS4. So at this point AS4 knows about two separate paths to reach **138.39.0.0/16**: one through AS2 and one through AS3. The MULTI-EXIT-DISCRIMINATOR attribute cannot be used here because there is exactly one connection between each pair of ASs, and MULTI-EXIT-DISCRIMINATORs are useful only between a pair of ASs that are directly connected in more than one place. Another reason that the MULTI-EXIT-DISCRIMINATOR attribute isn't sufficient in this case is that AS4 may want to control the path it selects for reaching the prefix. For example, assume that AS3 provides better service to AS1 than AS2, so AS4 may not want to send traffic to AS1 through AS2. AS4 can implement this preference by configuring the value of the LOCAL-PREF attribute assigned to prefixes heard from AS3 to be higher than prefixes heard from AS2. (As is discussed later in this chapter, the interpretation of the value of the

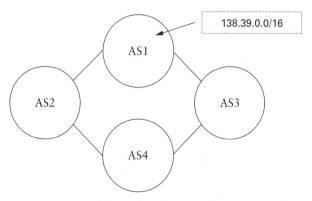

Figure 2-12 *Example topology with multiple paths*

LOCAL-PREF attribute is that the higher the value the more preferred the route.) The result of configuring the LOCAL-PREF values this way is that AS4 can be sure that it uses AS3 to reach the prefix.

The LOCAL-PREF attribute is the metric most often used in practice to express preferences for one set of paths over another.

The LOCAL-PREF attribute is type code 5 and is a well-known discretionary attribute. The length of the attribute is always four octets, and the encoding is an unsigned integer.

2.4.6 ATOMIC-AGGREGATE

The purpose of the ATOMIC-AGGREGATE attribute is to allow BGP speakers to inform each other about decisions they have made with respect to overlapping routes. For example, imagine that Router A hears both 138.39.0.0/16 and 138.39.12.0/24 from Router B and that the attributes associated with the two prefixes are different (for example, the AS-PATH isn't the same). If, for some reason, Router A is configured to use 138.39.0.0/16 but not 138.39.12.0/24, Router A should attach the ATOMIC-AGGREGATE attribute to the prefix when it advertises the prefix to other neighbors. When a BGP speaker receives a prefix with the ATOMIC-AGGREGATE attribute set, that BGP speaker must not take the prefix and de-aggregate it into any more specific entries in BGP. In the example presented here, if Router A advertised 138.39.0.0/16 to Router C with the ATOMIC-AGGREGATE attribute attached, Router C would know that the paths toward some subset of the address space described by the aggregate might traverse ASs not listed in the AS-PATH attribute.

The ATOMIC-AGGREGATE attribute is type code 6 and is a well-known discretionary attribute. The attribute has a zero length and therefore no value because the attribute is used basically as a flag indicating whether or not the prefix is an atomic aggregate; a prefix either is or is not an atomic aggregate, so no value is needed.

2.4.7 AGGREGATOR

If a BGP speaker performs aggregation on some of the address space it hears from some peers and then announces to others, it may choose to attach an AGGREGATOR attribute to the aggregated prefix to specify the AS and router that performed the aggregation.

The AGGREGATOR attribute is type code 7 and is an optional transitive attribute. The length of the attribute is always six, and it is encoded as a two-octet ASN followed by a four-octet IP address.

2.5 Internal Versus External BGP

To this point BGP has been presented only as an EGP, meaning that it has been presented as a routing protocol that runs between ASs. This operation between ASs is only one of the two uses of BGP. The pure EGP use of BGP that has been presented so far resembles the topology shown in Figure 2-13.

In this example we see that R3 in AS1 and R4 in AS2 have a BGP session between them so that R3 learns about AS2's routes and R4 learns about AS1's routes. The important element missing in this picture is an explanation of how R1 and R2 learn about AS2's routes and, similarly, how R5 learns about AS1's routes. In other words, how are prefixes learned by a single router in an AS via a BGP session distributed to the other routers in the AS? One possible way to do this is to inject into the IGP the prefixes learned via BGP from other ASs. Some smaller networks that do not need to carry a full routing table may take this approach. However, it simply doesn't work in the case of service providers that carry a full routing table because the volume of routes is far too large and the rate of change is too frequent; IGPs typically don't scale well enough to carry full Internet routing. There are several specific reasons that IGPs don't scale well enough to carry a full Internet routing table. The first reason is the computational complexity of calculating shortest paths. Other reasons stem from the tremendous increase in the amount of information in an LSP. The LSDB grows very

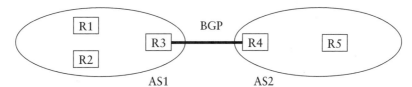

Figure 2-13 *Example topology for E-BGP versus I-BGP*

large, the LSPs become fragmented, and the job of flooding the LSPs creates a tremendous amount of control traffic. The preferred way of distributing externally learned prefixes within a network is through a use of BGP called **Internal BGP (I-BGP)**.

The pure EGP use of BGP is most accurately called **External BGP (E-BGP)**. E-BGP is used between ASs (for example, where two providers connect to each other or where a customer connects to its provider). I-BGP, on the other hand, is used *within* an AS (between two routers in the same AS), and it achieves the requirement of distributing routes learned through E-BGP to the rest of the routers in the AS.

I-BGP and E-BGP are the same protocol in the sense that they share the same message types (OPEN, UPDATE, KEEPALIVE, and NOTIFI-CATION), the same attribute types (AS-PATH, NEXT-HOP, and so on), and the same state machine. However, an important difference between I-BGP and E-BGP is that they have different rules about re-advertising prefixes. Specifically, the specification of BGP4 says that prefixes learned from an E-BGP neighbor can be advertised to an I-BGP neighbor and vice versa, but a prefix learned from an I-BGP neighbor cannot be advertised to another I-BGP neighbor. Consider Figure 2-14 for an explanation.

Note that this diagram is presented from R3's perspective and shows only the BGP connections relevant to it. Given the specification of BGP4, R3 can advertise prefixes learned from R4 to both R1 and R2. Furthermore, R3 can advertise to R4 any prefixes it learns from R1 and R2. However, R3 cannot advertise to R2 any prefixes that it learns from R1. This last point suggests the way in which Figure 2-14

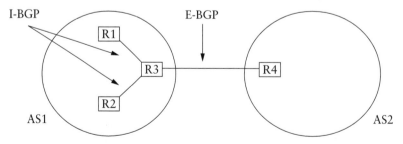

Figure 2-14 *Comparing I-BGP and E-BGP*

is incomplete. For R1 to reach prefixes injected into the I-BGP mesh by R2 (and vice versa), there must be an I-BGP connection directly between them. This direct I-BGP connection between R1 and R2 is not shown in Figure 2-14.

The reason BGP contains this rule about I-BGP readvertisement is to prevent looping routing announcement within an AS. Remember that BGP's mechanism for detecting looping routing announcements is the AS-PATH attribute. However, the AS-PATH is appended to only as routes cross AS boundaries, and in the case of I-BGP, the routes do not cross an AS boundary.

The major result of these rules about advertising prefixes between E-BGP and I-BGP neighbors is the need for a **full mesh** of I-BGP connections—in other words, there must be an I-BGP session between every pair of routers within an AS. Figure 2-15 shows an example of a full mesh.

Note carefully that this full mesh of I-BGP connections is completely independent of physical connectivity, so the fact that two routers have a direct I-BGP connection between them does not necessarily mean that the two routers are directly connected. In contrast, E-BGP sessions typically correspond to a physical link. When two ASs connect to each other, typically they have a circuit in place between two routers and those two routers speak E-BGP with each other. For example, the logical I-BGP topology shown in Figure 2-15 could be built on top of a physical topology as shown in Figure 2-16. So in this example, R4 and R5 have an I-BGP session directly between them even

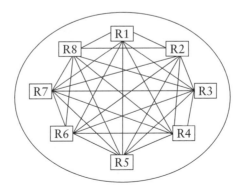

Figure 2-15 *Full mesh of I-BGP connections*

though they don't have a link directly between them. In this case R1 must forward the packets that are part of the I-BGP session. R1 doesn't actually participate in the I-BGP session between R4 and R5; it simply forwards packets and isn't even aware that some of the packets it forwards between R4 and R5 are part of a BGP session.

Another important feature in the context of E-BGP and I-BGP is to establish the degree of route preference. When a router injects a route for a particular prefix into the I-BGP mesh within an AS, it is that router's responsibility to establish the degree of preference for the route. The router may learn about the route via E-BGP, or it may learn about it through an internal mechanism such as static configuration or an IGP. Either way, the router establishes the degree of preference. If the router ends up advertising this route to other routers within the AS, this degree of preference is included in the LOCAL-PREF attribute. Because the routers within an AS have I-BGP sessions with each other, they all know the degree of preference for the routes each of those routers is injecting into I-BGP. Imagine that Router A learns a route for 138.39.0.0/16 through some mechanism and calculates the degree of preference for that route as 100. If Router A had previously learned a route for 138.39.0.0/16 through an I-BGP session with Router B, the action that Router A takes depends on the value of the LOCAL-PREF attribute of the route learned from Router B. If the route learned from Router B has a LOCAL-PREF higher than 100, Router B's route to the prefix is preferred and Router A will not inject its route into the I-BGP mesh. If, on the other hand, Router B's route has a LOCAL-PREF

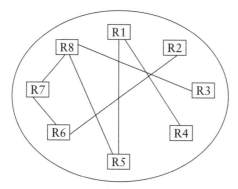

Figure 2-16 *Physical topology corresponding to I-BGP mesh*

lower than 100, Router A's route is preferred and Router A will inject its route into the I-BGP mesh. Because the routers are fully meshed in I-BGP, Router B will learn about Router A's route and will react by withdrawing its route, leaving only Router A's route, which is the preferred one.

2.6 BGP Route Selection Process

A major part of any routing protocol is the algorithm used to select which, if any, of the possible paths toward a prefix should be selected and installed in the forwarding table. The input to this route selection process is the set of all routes that have been learned and accepted by the local system. If there is only one route toward a particular prefix, it is obviously the route that is used. The interesting case is the existence of multiple routes for a given prefix. Note very carefully that having multiple routes for a given prefix means that the local system has learned about more than one route for the same prefix with the same prefix length. If the local system learned about two prefixes that overlap—but don't have identical prefix lengths—this does not satisfy having two routes for the same prefix. If, however, the local system has learned more than one route for the identical prefix, it uses the following tie-breaking rules to decide which one of the routes to use.

1. The route with the highest LOCAL-PREF value is selected first. This degree of preference could have been computed locally or could have been learned from another router. The value will have been computed locally for routes learned via an E-BGP session or for routes learned from sources such as an IGP or static configuration. The preference will have been learned from another router for routes learned from an I-BGP neighbor—specifically, the UPDATE message for that route will have contained a LOCAL-PREF attribute indicating the degree of preference. If this step selects exactly one route, the tie-breaking process is complete. If this step doesn't select exactly one route, the system goes to the next step.

2. The route with the shortest AS-PATH is selected. If this step selects exactly one route, the tie-breaking process is complete. If this step doesn't select exactly one route, the system goes to the next step.

3. If the local system is configured to take into account the value of the MULTI-EXIT-DISCRIMINATOR, and if the multiple routes were learned from the same neighboring AS, the route with the lowest MULTI-EXIT-DISCRIMINATOR value is selected.[1] If this step selects exactly one route, the tie-breaking process is complete. If this step doesn't select exactly one route, the system goes to the next step.

4. In this step the local system analyzes the NEXT-HOP attribute of each of the routes. The local system selects the route that has the minimum cost to the NEXT-HOP. Deciding on the cost for a NEXT-HOP typically involves looking into the IGP's database. If this step selects exactly one route, the tie-breaking process is complete. If this step doesn't select exactly one route, the system goes to the next step.

5. If all the routes were learned via I-BGP, the system goes to the next step. If exactly one of the routes was learned via E-BGP, that route is selected. If more than one route was learned via E-BGP, then the route learned from the E-BGP neighbor with the lowest BGP identifier is selected.

6. If all routes were learned via I-BGP, the route that was learned from the I-BGP neighbor with the lowest BGP identifier is selected.

The preceding list is probably even more complicated than it seems. The actual behavior of the route selection process in practice is not always intuitive. In spite of its complexity, this decision process is especially well understood by large providers because it has a profound impact on how their network is used both by customers and by providers that they peer with.

---

1. Note that the original version of the BGP specification wasn't specific about comparing routes when one has a MULTI-EXIT-DISCRIMINATOR and one doesn't. One implementation treats a missing MULTI-EXIT-DISCRIMINATOR as zero, whereas another treats it as the maximum value (four octets of 1s).

3

BGP Operations

Chapter 2 presents a rather sterile view of BGP's messages, attributes, rules, and so on. Although it is critical for protocol implementers to know and understand these kinds of details, it isn't as important to users of the protocol. The critical things for users of the protocol to understand are the ways that networks using BGP are configured, the way that BGP interacts with other parts of the system such as the IGP, the dynamics of the protocol's operation, and so on. These things are presented in this chapter—those elements of the protocol that are important in an operational sense.

Before we go into specifics of individual areas, let's draw a high-level picture illustrating all the major pieces of a small but practical network based on BGP. Figure 3-1 shows such a picture.

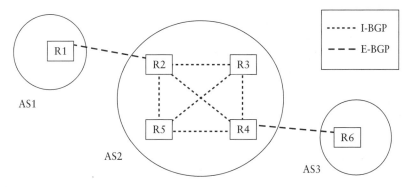

Figure 3-1 *Complete BGP example*

This picture is shown from the perspective of AS2, so only the routers in AS1 and AS3 that connect to AS2 are shown. In this figure we see that AS2 has four routers, each of which has an I-BGP connection to all other routers. AS1 and AS2 are connected via an E-BGP connection between R1 and R2. AS2 and AS3 are connected via an E-BGP session between R4 and R6. On the E-BGP session between AS1 and AS2, R1 advertises routes for prefixes within AS1, and R2 advertises routes for prefixes within both AS2 and AS3. R2 will have learned routes for prefixes within AS3 via the I-BGP session with R4. R4 will have learned these routes directly from R6 via the E-BGP session. Finally, R4 advertises to R6 routes for prefixes within both AS2 and AS1. Remember that one of the required path attributes is the AS-PATH, so as routes are passed between ASs, the AS-PATH attribute is updated. For example, if AS2 learns a route for **138.39.0.0/16** from AS1, while the route is carried in AS2's I-BGP mesh it will have an AS-PATH attribute with a value of "AS1." Furthermore, if AS2 ends up advertising that prefix to AS3, the route that R6 learns will have an AS-PATH attribute with a value of "AS2 AS1."

3.1 IGP Interaction

One of the difficulties of understanding the operational nature of BGP is understanding the interaction between BGP and other parts of the system. For large backbones, the IGP is typically one of the most complicated and potentially fragile pieces; therefore, the interaction between BGP and the IGP is usually one of the most interesting.

The interaction between the IGP and E-BGP tends to be completely different from the interaction between the IGP and I-BGP. The need to configure I-BGP and E-BGP quite differently accounts for the difference. Consider the topology shown in Figure 3-2.

In this example AS1 and AS2 are connected via a physical link between R1 and R2. The dynamic routing part of the connection is accomplished through an E-BGP session over this physical link between R1 and R2. Within AS2 there are four routers, physically connected with four point-to-point links, thus forming a ring. Between these four routers in AS2 there is a full mesh of I-BGP connections.

Remember that BGP runs over a TCP connection. TCP connections are identified by the combination of the source and destination IP

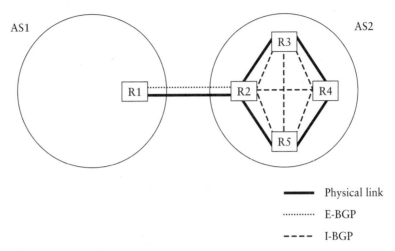

Figure 3-2 *Example IGP interaction*

addresses and the source and destination TCP port numbers. For this reason, the exact addresses used for a BGP session turn out to be important. For hosts, which typically have only one address, the choice of which address to use is usually easy, for obvious reasons. However, a router often has as many addresses as it does interfaces, so the choice isn't as obvious. Consider Figure 3-3, which is an expansion of R1 and R2 and the link between them from Figure 3-2. Note that the addresses shown in Figure 3-3 are the full 32-bit IP addresses, and the significance of the /30 is to indicate the mask of the link to which the interfaces are connected.

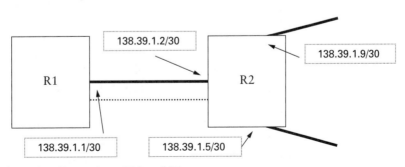

Figure 3-3 *Expansion of R1 and R2*

In this example we see that one of R1's addresses is **138.39.1.1/30**, and it corresponds to the point-to-point link between R1 and R2. In reality, R1 would have more interfaces and thus more addresses, but for simplicity they are not shown in this example. R2 has three interfaces and thus three addresses. The first address is **138.39.1.2/30**, and it corresponds to R2's side of the point-to-point link between R1 and R2. Note the relationship between the two ends of the point-to-point link: they are on the same IP subnet, which makes sense because R1 and R2 are directly connected via that link. The second address on R2 is **138.39.1.5/30**, and, referencing Figure 3-2, it corresponds to the link between R2 and R5. The third address on R2 is **138.39.1.9/30**, and it corresponds to the link between R2 and R3.

For the E-BGP connection between R1 and R2, the endpoints of the TCP connection are **138.39.1.1** and **138.39.1.2**. If the link between R1 and R2 went down, both routers would know and would mark the interfaces as down. As soon as one of the routers would try to send a message (such as an UPDATE or a KEEPALIVE) via the BGP session, the router would see that it could no longer reach the destination. At that point the BGP session would be considered down, and each router would remove from its routing and forwarding tables any routes that it learned via that E-BGP session. This behavior intuitively matches the purpose of E-BGP. Specifically, because the point of E-BGP is to interconnect ASs and because the connectivity between ASs is sparse relative to the connectivity within an AS. Therefore, if a link between ASs goes down, administrators of those ASs would want the E-BGP session to go down.

I-BGP, on the other hand, is quite different. Consider Figure 3-4. In this diagram we see R1, R2, and R3 in the same AS. Each router has a direct physical connection to the other two. In addition to the physical connection, each router has an I-BGP session with the other two. We just learned that the endpoints of TCP connections for E-BGP sessions are the addresses of the physical interfaces over which the E-BGP session runs. So the question here is which addresses should be used for I-BGP sessions.

Imagine what would happen if the same approach were taken with I-BGP sessions as with E-BGP sessions and that the endpoints of the TCP connection for the I-BGP session between R1 and R2 were **138.39.1.1** and **138.39.1.2**. This approach works fine as long as there

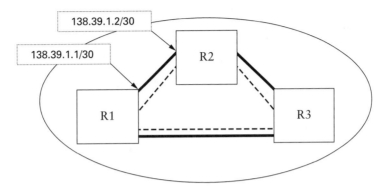

Figure 3-4 *Example of I-BGP topology*

are no failures. However, during link failures, there can be unacceptable failure conditions. Imagine that the link between R1 and R2 goes down. In that situation, although traffic between R1 and R2 cannot flow on the link directly between them, it is still a requirement that R1 and R2 be able to exchange traffic, so the indirect path through R3 must be used. Meeting this demand requires that I-BGP and E-BGP have different conventions with respect to the TCP endpoints used.

Let us analyze in detail what would happen if I-BGP used the same convention as E-BGP with respect to the TCP endpoints used. Assuming the R1-R2 link is up, if R1 learns a route via E-BGP and advertises that route to R2 via I-BGP using a NEXT-HOP of **138.39.1.1**, R2 will forward traffic toward the associated prefix by forwarding that traffic across the point-to-point link between R2 and R1. This works fine because the R1-R2 link is up, but the approach breaks down in the face of link failures. Imagine that the point-to-point link between R1 and R2 goes down. The result is that the **138.39.1.0/30** subnet becomes unreachable. As a result, a TCP connection cannot be established using an address from that subnet as an endpoint. The result of this from a networkwide perspective is that R1 and R2 will not have connectivity to routes that each of them injects into the I-BGP mesh. This is unacceptable from an operational standpoint because R1 and R2 still have a viable path between them (the path that goes through R3), so the protocol should adapt to the failure rather than just stop working.

The difference in approach between E-BGP and I-BGP that deals with this failure scenario is shown in Figure 3-5 by expanding the detail about the I-BGP session between R1 and R2 from Figure 3-4.

In this diagram we again see the point-to-point link between R1 and R2 along with the associated addresses. We also see the I-BGP session between R1 and R2. But in this diagram we also see the addition of the addresses **138.39.128.1** and **138.39.128.5**, and the I-BGP session is drawn between these newly introduced addresses. The newly introduced addresses correspond to **virtual interface**s within R1 and R2. These interfaces aren't associated with a physical link or a hardware interface. In practice, these interfaces are most often called **loopback interface**s. By having the I-BGP session run between the loopback interfaces, the I-BGP session will stay up as long as there is a path between R1 and R2.

Saying that I-BGP sessions run between loopback interfaces explains conceptually how I-BGP sessions work, but that explanation also introduces more questions. The fundamental issue is about what is and what is not directly reachable. Specifically, because R1 must open a TCP connection to **138.39.128.5** (R2's loopback address) to start the I-BGP session with R2, R1 must know how to reach that address. Furthermore, this reachability must be symmetric, so R2 must

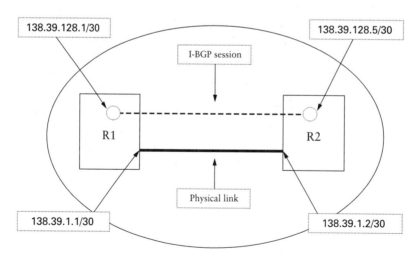

Figure 3-5 *Dissection of I-BGP session*

know how to reach 138.39.128.1 (R1's loopback address). Because R1 is not directly connected to an interface on the 138.39.128.4/30 subnet (and because R2 is not directly connected to 138.39.128.0/30), some type of routing is needed. It is here that the IGP comes into play.

An IGP is used to route the addresses corresponding to the loopback addresses. After all the routers in the AS know how to reach all the other routers' loopback addresses, the I-BGP sessions can be established and routes can be exchanged.

3.2 Routing Policy and Transit Versus Nontransit

When a BGP speaker receives an UPDATE message containing some number of routes, the BGP speaker is not obligated to accept any or all of the routes. Furthermore, if that BGP speaker chooses to accept one or more of the advertised routes, it makes no implication about the preference the BGP speaker will give those routes over other routes for the same prefix heard from other sources. Said another way, the decision about which routes to accept from a neighbor and the preference with which those routes should be treated is a local decision. This is the role of routing policy. Another part of routing policy is to decide which set of routes should be advertised to each BGP neighbor.

The decision about which routes to accept from and advertise to various BGP neighbors has a profound impact on what traffic crosses a network. Routing policy is used to enforce business agreements made between two or more parties. Consider Figure 3-6.

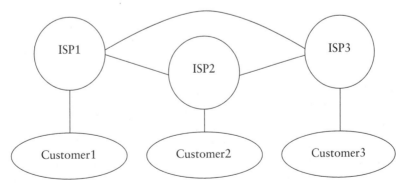

Figure 3-6 *Routing policy and transit explanation*

In this diagram we see three ISPs and three customers. ISP1, ISP2, and ISP3 are directly connected to one another via a physical link and a corresponding E-BGP session. Customer1 is connected to ISP1 via a physical link and corresponding E-BGP session. Similarly, Customer2 is connected to ISP2, and Customer3 is connected to ISP3. Each customer pays its ISP for connectivity to the Internet. At one level this statement seems trivial and obvious. But at another level it is much more powerful because when an ISP provides Internet connectivity to its customers, it is providing connectivity to customers of other ISPs. Those ISPs and customers could be on the other side of the planet. At the same time that an ISP provides such a large degree of connectivity, it must also prevent its resources from being used inappropriately. An example of inappropriate use would be Customer1 reaching Customer3 by going through ISP2; in this case parties that don't pay ISP2 would use ISP2's resources. This stands in contrast to Customer1 reaching Customer3 by going through only ISP1 and ISP3, when the ISP's resources would be used by traffic going to or coming from a customer. It is these exchanges that routing policy enforces. The kind of service that an ISP provides to its customer is called **transit service** because that ISP is willing to allow traffic to transit its backbone on the way to other parts of the Internet. The kind of service that ISP1 provides to ISP2 (who doesn't pay ISP1) is called **nontransit service** because ISP1 is willing to accept traffic from ISP2 only if the traffic is bound for one of its customers.

Understanding both the BGP mechanisms and the need for routing policy, it is worth examining in detail how routing policy is used to enforce the administrative policy described in the preceding paragraph. For simplicity we will look at this from the perspective of ISP1: what it must do with respect to its customer and the other ISPs in order to enforce a sensible routing policy. Because the service that ISP1 provides to Customer1 is Internet connectivity, ISP1 must make sure that other ISPs (and, by extension, customers of those other ISPs) can reach Customer1. For this reason, ISP1 must be sure to announce routes for any prefixes used by Customer1 to both ISP2 and ISP3. Having ensured that other parties can reach Customer1, the other half of Internet connectivity is to ensure that Customer1 can reach other parties. ISP1 must be sure to announce effectively all of the routes it knows about to Customer1. What ISP1 must be careful not to do, however, is to announce ISP2's routes to ISP3. If ISP1 were to announce ISP2's routes to ISP3, ISP1 might be used for traffic going between Customer2 and Customer3, and that is the thing that we were trying to prevent.

Earlier we said that ISP1 will announce to ISP2 and ISP3 any routes heard from Customer1. This topic deserves a little more attention. Although it certainly is true that ISP1 must announce the prefixes used by Customer1 so that other ISPs can reach Customer1, that doesn't necessarily equate to ISP1 believing everything announced by Customer1 and arbitrarily reannouncing it. In fact, because ISP1 advertises Customer1's information into the global Internet routing mesh, ISP1 needs to take great care that what is announced is legitimate. For this reason, ISP1 might filter what it accepts from Customer1 based on static or semistatic information about the prefixes being used by Customer1.

3.3 Notes About Practice

In reality, most customers of an ISP do not use BGP. Instead, most customers are routed with static configuration. Specifically, the ISP's router to which the customer is connected is configured with the prefix used by that customer. It is also configured to announce a route for that prefix into BGP. As a result, the customer is connected to the ISP, and thus the Internet, without having to speak BGP itself. In these instances when a route for the prefix used by the customer is seen elsewhere in the Internet's routing mesh, the AS-PATH attribute on the route indicates that the origin AS is the ISP and not the customer itself. This statement matches the earlier one that the customer doesn't speak BGP, which would also imply that the customer doesn't have an AS number that identifies it.

Currently, the two primary ways that ISPs handle routing for customers is static configuration and dynamic routing with BGP. Of these two, static routing is more common than BGP. In rare circumstances an ISP will include its customers' address space in its IGP. This arrangement is potentially risky for the ISP because IGPs can be fragile in the face of only a single badly configured router. In other circumstances an ISP may use a *small* IGP that is limited to doing the dynamic routing with the customer. The most common example of this is using RIP

(Routing Information Protocol) on the point-to-point link between the ISP and its customer to allow the customer to dynamically advertise its prefix(es) to the ISP. This type of configuration doesn't have the same disadvantages of the other approach (the inclusion of the customers in the IGP), but the practical reality is that it is much less common than either BGP or static routing.

As stated earlier, route aggregation is critical to the scalability of Internet routing. For this reason, most customers of an ISP use address space from an aggregate belonging to the ISP. Customers that are statically routed as described earlier probably won't have their individual prefix announced into the Internet; instead, that prefix is part of the aggregate, which is announced by the ISP into the Internet.

For those customers that speak BGP, those customers usually don't carry every single route in the Internet. Carrying all routes in the Internet is not typically necessary for subscribers and has traditionally required expensive configurations of expensive routers. The most common case involves the subscriber carrying a default route used to forward all nonlocal traffic to the ISP.

3.4 A Singly Homed Subscriber

This section describes the way that a typical BGP customer connects to its ISP. Consider Figure 3-7. In this diagram we see that AS1, the subscriber, is a customer of AS2, the provider. AS1 has a network with some topology and uses the **138.39.2.0/23** prefix for address space. AS2 presumably has some topology itself, although for simplicity it is not shown. There is a physical link connecting AS1 to AS2 via routers R1 and R2. This link is the subscriber's access circuit. In today's Internet, this circuit could be anywhere from 64 kbps to 622 Mbps. Typically there is a correlation between the speed of the access circuit and the need to use BGP, so in reality the access circuit in this situation would be at least a T-1 (1.544 Mbps) and could even be a DS-3 (45 Mbps) or more. Regardless of speed, the point of the circuit is to connect a port on R1 to a port on R2. With that physical resource in place, R1 and R2 can establish an E-BGP session for dynamic routing so that traffic can go between the two ASs.

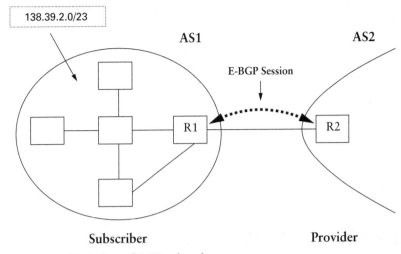

Figure 3-7 *Singly homed BGP subscriber*

The configuration of R1 would include specifying that it should establish a BGP session with R2 in a particular AS and at a particular IP address. Similarly, R2's configuration would specify a BGP session with R1 in a particular AS and at a particular IP address. The configuration of R1's routing policy would have R1 announce the **138.39.2.0/23** prefix over the BGP session to R2. To do this, R1 may need to aggregate a number of more-specifics within the prefix. R2's routing policy configuration may include filtering the routes that it hears from R1 so that R2 accepts advertisements only for the **138.39.2.0/23** prefix. This demonstrates how simple this example is: typically, the number of prefixes exchanged between subscriber and provider is much greater than one. In addition to the configuration of policy for routing information flowing from R1 to R2, there may be policy configured for the flow in the opposite direction. For example, R2 may filter the routes that it advertises to R1 so that R1 doesn't have to carry a full Internet routing table. Instead (or in addition), R1 may filter the routes that it hears from R2. Filtering of routes by R1 assures R1 that it accepts only the routes that it wants instead of all of R2's routes.

3.5 A Multihomed Subscriber

Multihoming has become a frequently discussed issue in the past few years. Multihoming refers to a single network having more than one connection to the Internet.[1] The typical motivation for multihoming is to improve reliability and performance. The reliability comes from the fact that a multihomed site can accommodate a single circuit or router failure without losing Internet connectivity. The performance improvement comes from the fact that the site's bandwidth to the Internet is the sum of the bandwidths of all circuits. Performance is increased only if more than one link is used at a time; otherwise, the maximum performance would be the bandwidth of the one link being used at a given instant. The term **load sharing** is used loosely to refer to this use of multiple links in parallel. Some people in the industry use the term **load balancing** to refer to an even split of traffic across the multiple links. Except for very low-level mechanisms such as inverse multiplexers (IMUXs) and Multi-Link Point-to-Point Protocol (PPP) (both of which are described a little later), achieving this kind of load balancing is almost impossible. The primary reasons are the dynamics of Internet traffic and the coarse granularity of control offered by routing protocols such as BGP.

Note that, as a practical reality, a customer is almost never exclusively concerned with reliability. If a customer pays for two Internet connections, the customer will want to use both connections, even if all the traffic could be carried on a single link. For this reason, this section approaches multihoming situations in which both reliability and performance are requirements.

Two issues often discussed in multihoming situations are **route symmetry** and **packet reordering**. In symmetric routing, the path that Node A takes to get to Node B is the same path (in reverse) that Node B takes to get to Node A. If the paths are different, the path is asymmetric. Conventional wisdom is that symmetric paths are better than asymmetric paths, but in reality most routing between large providers,

---

1. The term *multihoming* is also often used in narrower terms to refer to a host with more than one interface. This book does not discuss host-level multihoming.

especially for networks geographically far from each other, is asymmetric. Packet reordering is of potentially greater concern. The essence of multihoming is the existence of multiple paths to a particular network. Depending on how the infrastructure deals with these multiple paths, it is possible for observed performance to actually decrease. TCP uses a number of algorithms to control and avoid congestion and to maximize performance without hurting the network. One of these algorithms, fast retransmit, is triggered by out-of-order delivery of data packets. The conclusion is that, in a multihoming situation, an attempt should be made not to reorder packets within a given TCP flow.

Being multihomed is intrinsically complicated. It is not terribly well handled by BGP, and it interacts in complex ways with aggregation and address allocation policies. This complexity must be recognized up front by an organization wishing to multihome so that a routing plan can be developed. Some types of multihoming are more run-of-the-mill than others, although all of them should be approached with care. It is possible that some requirements either cannot be met or can be met only by an unconventional method that might work only in a few special situations.

Another note about multihoming is that routing is only one of the considerations. Other technical items that should be considered are addressing, DNS, and aggregation.

As alluded to earlier, using BGP in multihoming situations is not an off-the-shelf use of the protocol. Instead, it requires a fair amount of thought and careful configuration. Having said that, however, it is also true that there are few alternatives to BGP in multihoming situations. As described in Section 3.3, the two current approaches used by ISPs to do routing for their customers' prefixes are static routing and BGP. Static routing works perfectly well for singly homed customers, but it does not work so well for multihomed ones. To understand why, consider Figure 3-8.

In this figure we see that Customer has two links to ISP1: one to R2 and one to R3. Within ISP1, R2 and R3 are **access routers** because they terminate access circuits from customers as well as circuits that connect ISP1 to other providers. R1 is considered a **core router**, and it connects to access routers and to other core routers. Finally, we see that R2 has a connection to an interconnect point where ISP1 can exchange

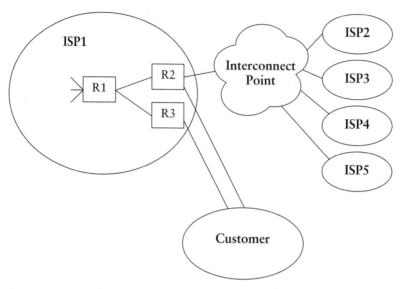

Figure 3-8 *Example multihoming with static routing*

traffic with ISP2, ISP3, ISP4, and ISP5. If Customer were statically routed on both R2 and R3, the result could be that much more traffic would be sent to Customer over the link from R2 than the link from R3. Because R2 connects to the interconnect point, it receives significantly more traffic relative to R3, and any of that traffic bound for Customer will go via the R2 link because of the static route configuration. If ISP1 were very large compared with the other ISPs, this behavior might not be a problem. However, the point of this example is to demonstrate that static routing does not offer much flexibility in directing traffic for a multihomed site, and the traffic behavior seen by Customer could change dramatically because of changes made within the ISP.

The following two sections describe some of the challenges presented by multihoming and some approaches for using BGP to deal with these challenges. It would be easy to write a whole book on multihoming and still not cover all the issues and possible configurations. The goal is to present the major high-level issues of which a person considering multihoming should be aware. To put various multihoming strategies into practice, an Internet subscriber should consult with his or her provider.

There are two very basic types of multihomed sites: sites with two or more connections to the same provider and sites with two or more connections to more than one provider. Each type has its own set of challenges and complexities. The second type has the potential for having a wider scope because the site's multihoming may be known throughout the Internet and not only between the site and its provider.

3.5.1 Multihoming to a Single Provider

Sites that are multihomed to a single provider can be subcategorized along several dimensions. First is the topology (the routers on which the circuits terminate in both the provider's and the subscriber's network, and the position of those routers within the respective networks). Other dimensions include overlapping areas of addressing as well as aggregation, the resources of routers within the site, and the proportionality of traffic to and from the site.

Figure 3-9 presents a simple topology. Here we see that the ISP and Customer are connected via two parallel links between the same two routers. In this example it is likely that the multihoming can be handled without BGP. At the lowest layers, it may be possible to use a pair of IMUXs. An IMUX is a device that takes one serial stream of bits from the router and equally divides the bits between two or more circuits (and vice versa). Another potential solution at a slightly higher layer is

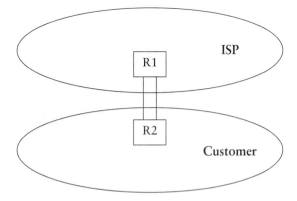

Figure 3-9 *Parallel links between one pair of routers*

to use Multi-Link PPP, a link-layer protocol that allows multiple links to be bundled together so that the IP layer sees only one virtual link. These two approaches work regardless of what happens at higher layers. In fact, they even work for static routing.

There is a third, more complicated approach for this situation involving only one BGP peering session, although it makes certain assumptions about addressing and traffic. To fully explain this approach, additional detail is added to Figure 3-10.

In this figure we see R1 and R2 connected via two physical links. On R1, the IP addresses of the physical interfaces are 192.1.1.1/30 and 192.1.1.5/30, whereas on R2 the IP addresses of the physical interfaces are 192.1.1.2/30 and 192.1.1.6/30. (Note that the addresses of the two interfaces on the same physical link are on the same IP subnet.) In addition, R1 and R2 have loopback addresses 192.1.128.1/30 and 192.1.128.5/30, respectively. If R1 and R2 both support some kind of load sharing in the face of equal cost routes, then R1 can be configured

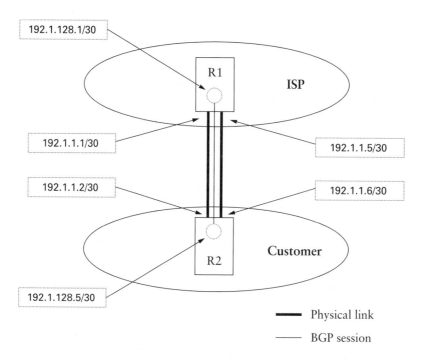

Figure 3-10 *Detail of parallel links between one pair of routers*

with two static routes for R2's loopback address, and, similarly, R2 can be configured with two static routes for R1's loopback address. For example, R1 can be configured with static routes so that the next hops for 192.1.128.5/30 are 192.1.1.2 and 192.1.1.6. The E-BGP peering session can be configured on R1 and R2 so that the endpoints of the underlying TCP connection as well as the value of the NEXT-HOP attributes in routes advertised are the loopback addresses. Imagine that R2 advertises two routes—10.0.0.0/8 and 192.168.0.0/16—to R1, both with a NEXT-HOP value of R2's loopback address. Assume that R1 accepts and selects both of these routes and then needs to install forwarding entries for them. When R1 processes the first route, R1 will see that the NEXT-HOP (192.1.128.5) is an address that it cannot directly reach; R2's loopback address is not directly connected to R1. As a result, to install the forwarding entries R1 must do a **recursive lookup** to see how it gets to R2's loopback address. It is here that the static routes get used. This recursive lookup will yield two results (192.1.1.2 and 192.1.1.6)—one for each of the two links. The way routers behave at this point is vendor-specific, but a reasonable behavior is to randomly choose one of the paths. Imagine that R1 chooses the first path and so installs a forwarding entry for 10.0.0.0/8 pointing out of the first link. Next, R1 processes the advertisement for 192.168.0.0/16. The process will basically be the same, although let's assume that, because the choice of parallel path is random, R1 installs a forwarding entry for this prefix pointing out of the second link.[2] As a result, both links are used and some degree of load sharing is achieved. Furthermore, if one of the links is down, the static route pointing out of the down link will not be considered, so reliability is achieved.

As mentioned earlier, this approach makes a number of assumptions. First, because it relies on a somewhat random behavior, the load sharing is probabilistic and therefore is most effective when there are a large number of prefixes exchanged (greater than the two prefixes in

---

2. Keep in mind that this behavior of installing a single forwarding entry based on the recursive lookup is only one possible behavior. The behavior may change from vendor to vendor and even between two products of the same vendor. Another possible behavior is for two forwarding entries for each prefix to be installed, and the randomization of the link taken may happen at the time of forwarding.

this example). Another assumption is that the amount of traffic is the same for two different prefixes. If much more traffic is destined for one of the prefixes rather than the other, the degree of load sharing will suffer. This concern also lessens as the number of prefixes increases.

In analyzing these kinds of multihoming situations, it is important not to get stuck thinking in one direction. For example, so far we have considered only the flow of traffic from ISP to Customer and have not yet considered the opposite direction. Before considering complex configurations, we should reflect for a moment on whether the complexity is worth it. The vast majority of traffic in the Internet currently is HTTP traffic for Web access. One characteristic of HTTP traffic is that it is very asymmetric. Specifically, an HTTP client sends a small amount of data to the server (a request for a Web page), and the server responds with a potentially large amount of data (a lot of text, large graphics, and so on). If we assume that Customer from Figure 3-9 is a typical user site with mostly HTTP clients, the amount of traffic going from Customer to ISP is only a fraction of the amount of traffic going in the opposite direction. For this reason, there may be little value in deploying complex configurations to optimize the path that traffic takes from Customer to ISP.

If Customer sends enough traffic to ISP to warrant trying to achieve some degree of load sharing, there are a number of possibilities. First, if either the IMUX or Multi-Link PPP solution is used, excellent load sharing will automatically be achieved in both directions. Using the E-BGP loopback peering just described, the mechanism works in the same way from Customer to ISP as it does from ISP to Customer. So the degree of load sharing from Customer to ISP depends on the number of routes that Customer learns from the ISP. If the ISP advertises only a default route to Customer, it is difficult to achieve much load sharing because there is only a single forwarding entry installed.[3] If it is necessary for Customer to receive a number of routes in order to achieve some kind of load sharing, Customer can ask ISP to send either a full routing table (assuming that ISP itself has it) or a subset of a full

---

3. Again, this depends on the behavior of the routers. If a router supports a forwarding entry for a prefix (such as a default route) pointing out of two interfaces and can do something such as alternating the link used, some load sharing may be achieved.

routing table. Customer must consider the capability of its router R2 because carrying a full routing table has traditionally required a modern router, with respect to the amount of memory and scalability of its software.

Another possible topology is shown in Figure 3-11. In this diagram we see that the two links no longer go between a single pair of routers as in the preceding example. Instead, from ISP's router R1 there are two links going to two different routers—R2 and R3—in Customer. The ability to do load sharing from ISP to Customer depends on addressing within Customer and on the location of traffic sources and sinks within Customer. In this example Customer is shown as using prefixes **138.39/16** and **204.70/16**. If the amount of traffic going to these two networks is roughly equal, then a reasonable multi-homing strategy might be to use the R1-R2 link for traffic going to **138.39/16** and the R1-R3 link for traffic going to **204.70/16**. You can implement this by having Customer include MULTI-EXIT-DISCRIMINATORs on the two occurrences of each route, with the lowest MULTI-EXIT-DISCRIMINATOR being set on the path that is primary for that prefix. Another option is for ISP to set the LOCAL-PREF differently, which covers load sharing from ISP to Customer, although the other direction must also be considered. Assume that the topology in Customer closest to R2 produces about the same amount of traffic as the topology closest to R3. If two default routes are advertised within Customer, then a closest exit policy will produce reasonable load sharing.

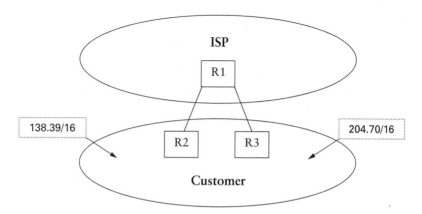

Figure 3-11 *Same router in ISP, different router in Customer*

If the assumptions made in the preceding example are not true, achieving very good load sharing may be much more difficult. For example, if Customer announces only a single prefix, typically the result will be that only one of the links is used at a time from ISP to Customer. Preventing this might necessitate breaking up the prefix into more-specifics to gain finer granularity of control. Also, if the amount of traffic produced by the areas of topology closest to R2 and R3, respectively, isn't roughly equal then the loading of the links from Customer to ISP could be greatly different. Preventing this might necessitate Customer getting a significant number of routes and coming up with a configuration that preferred some routes out of one link and other routes out of the other. Part of the point of this discussion is that a network designer should consider the things that make multihoming both easy and hard when deciding on topologies of inter-domain links.

Yet another example of a multihoming topology is shown in Figure 3-12.

In this example we see two links from different routers in ISP terminating on the same router within Customer. For load sharing in the direction from ISP to Customer, the situation is almost identical to the preceding example. Specifically, if the amount of traffic going to the two prefixes is about equal, using the R1-R3 link for traffic going to **138.39/16** and the R2-R3 link for traffic going to **204.70/16** could result in quite good load sharing. Load sharing for traffic going from Customer to ISP could be done in one of two ways. First, R3 could

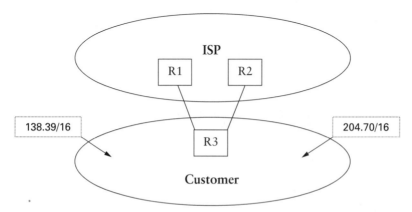

Figure 3-12 *Different routers in ISP, same router in Customer*

alternate the link it uses when sending packets to ISP. Although this results in quite good load sharing on the two links, it also has a relatively high probability of introducing packet reordering unless R3 has features that prevent it. The second approach for load sharing from Customer to ISP requires R3 to learn about more than only a default route from ISP. If R3 learned about many routes from ISP via the E-BGP sessions with both R1 and R2 and preferred some of those routes out of one link and some out of the other, load sharing might be quite good. This second solution is a broad category, and there are many possible ways to accomplish it. Depending on how large the ISP is, one possibility would be for the ISP to advertise all of its customer's routes on the R1-R3 link but advertise only default on the R2-R3 link. If about the same amount of traffic goes from Customer to ISP as goes from Customer to the rest of the Internet, this approach would result in good load sharing. If ISP isn't very large, it wouldn't result in good load sharing. Another option would be for Customer to request full routes via the R1 E-BGP session but hear only a default route from the R2 E-BGP session. In addition, R3 could apply a policy to the E-BGP session with R1 so that only routes with a particular AS-PATH would be accepted. The goal is to build the policy so that the amount of traffic toward the prefixes accepted by the filter should be about equal to the amount of traffic that ends up using the default route.

One final example multihoming topology is shown in Figure 3-13.

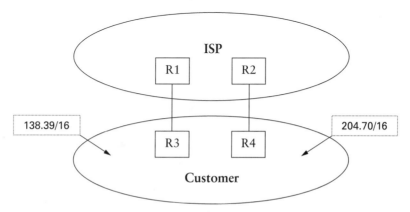

Figure 3-13 *Different routers in ISP, different routers in Customer*

The example shown here is the most reliable because no equipment is shared between the two links. The approach that can be taken in this situation for load sharing from Customer to ISP is the same as the approach presented in Figure 3-11. The reason is that, from Customer's perspective, there is no difference between the two topologies. For similar reasons, the approach taken for load sharing from ISP to Customer is the same as the approach presented in Figure 3-12.

3.5.2 Multihoming to More Than One Provider

Many of the same issues that complicate multihoming to a single provider also complicate multihoming to more than one provider, although in the latter the complexity might happen on a larger scale. In other words, when a site is multiply connected to a single provider, only the one site and the one provider are aware of the multihoming. However, when a site is multiply connected to more than one provider, the knowledge of the multihoming may be present across the whole Internet.

Although the theoretical issue of multihoming to more than one provider has at least as many components as multihoming to a single provider, the major issues for the former are addressing and aggregation. Consider Figure 3-14.

In this figure we see Customer multihomed to ISP1 and ISP2. ISP1, ISP2, and ISP3 all connect to one another. The question is how Customer should deal with the fact that it is multihomed to both ISP1 and ISP2. The first issue is the address space used by Customer, which ends up being critical for the load sharing from the ISPs to Customer. Customer has several possible approaches for addressing its network,

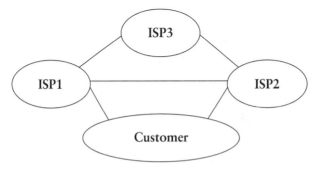

Figure 3-14 *Multihoming to ISP1 and ISP2*

where the main difference between the approaches is the address space used. The options are as follows:

1. Delegated to it by ISP1
2. Delegated to it by ISP2
3. Delegated to it by both ISP1 and ISP2
4. Obtained independently from an address registry

Each of these options has advantages and disadvantages for different parts of the Internet. In the following few paragraphs we describe the high points of each approach.

If Customer uses address space delegated to it by ISP1, ISP1's aggregation is not broken—that is, Customer uses a more-specific prefix out of ISP1's aggregate and ISP1 can announce only the aggregate to ISP2 and ISP3. For example, imagine that ISP1 has the block **138.39/16** and Customer uses **138.39.1/24**. In this case Customer would announce **138.39.1/24** to ISP1, and ISP1 would be able to aggregate that into **138.39/16** and announce only the aggregate to ISP2 and ISP3. Customer would also announce **138.39.1/24** to ISP2, although for ISP2 the address space is not aggregatable, so ISP2 passes the /24 to ISP1 and ISP3. Look at this from ISP3's perspective. Whether this would result in good load sharing from ISP1 and ISP2 to Customer depends on whether ISP1 does any internal aggregation and on the relative sizes of ISP1, ISP2, and ISP3. In the situation just described, the prefixes that ISP2 and ISP3 know about are **138.39.1/24**, corresponding to the ISP2-Customer link, and **138.39/16**, corresponding to the ISP1-ISP2 and ISP1-ISP3 links. Because CIDR requires a longest-match paradigm to be used, ISP2 and ISP3 will both get to Customer via the ISP2-Customer link. The longer prefix becomes something of a traffic magnet, so to speak. This isn't necessarily a problem, though, because if Customer gets as much traffic from ISP1 as it gets from ISP2 and ISP3 put together, the load sharing could be quite good. However, if ISP2 and ISP3 together send substantially more traffic to Customer than ISP1, the resulting load sharing can be quite poor. Note that the path that ISP1 itself takes to reach Customer isn't even guaranteed to be the ISP1-Customer link. Imagine that, rather than carry the /24 through its whole AS, ISP1 assigns an aggregate such as **138.39.0/19** to the access router terminating Customer's circuit, and the /19 is what is carried in I-BGP. This arrangement still allows ISP1 to announce only **138.39/16** to ISP2 and ISP3, and it also allows the internal routing table to be smaller than if it carried every individual customer's /24. The point is that if ISP1 learns the prefix **138.39.1/24** from ISP2, it may be a longer match than the prefix it has for its own customer, and ISP1 may not use the ISP1-Customer link. Most likely, this would be a problem, so ISP1 would need to configure the access router terminating Customer's circuit to inject the actual /24 into the I-BGP mesh.

If Customer uses address space delegated to it by ISP2, the behavior is analogous to the behavior in the first example except that ISP1 will be the ISP to announce the more-specific route and attract traffic to it. Remember that this approach can work quite well depending on the relative size of the providers involved, so the load sharing may be quite good if ISP1's address space is used but not very good if ISP2's address space is used.

One side note should be made about these first two addressing options. In describing the flow of routing announcements, an assumption was made that, for example, Customer's announcement of **138.39.1/24** to ISP2 would be accepted, as would ISP2's subsequent announcement of that prefix to ISP1 and ISP3. This is not necessarily the case. Starting in about 1995, some providers implemented a routing policy that would reject routes for prefixes with lengths longer than the classful route would have been and also would reject routes for prefixes with lengths greater than /19 for newly assigned address space. In other words, because **138.39.1/24** is out of the natural Class B space (a /16), the /24 would be rejected. The second part of the policy would reject routes such as **207.1.8/21** but, for historical purposes, would allow **192.1.1/24**. The people who implemented these routing policies claimed to be doing it to encourage better aggregation throughout the Internet. Although it was a contentious issue then and continues to be one now, it is also true that these policies probably improved aggregation. The point of this discussion is that these filters must be kept in mind when you're designing a multihoming strategy because it can have significant effects on the resulting traffic flow and load sharing.

The third addressing option is for Customer to use address space delegated to it by both ISP1 and ISP2. From the perspective of aggregation, this option has the potential for being a very good one. For example, imagine that Customer is assigned **138.39.1/24** from ISP1 and **204.70.1/24** from ISP2. Because both of these prefixes are from an aggregate belonging to both ISPs, the ISPs can continue to announce only the aggregate to, for example, ISP3. In this case, the degree of load sharing from ISP1 and ISP2 to Customer depends on the amount of traffic destined for the two prefixes; if the amount of traffic destined for the two is about the same, the load sharing toward the customer can be quite good. If the amount of traffic is not equal, the load sharing could be very poor; because ISP2 hasn't even learned about the 138.39.1/24 prefix from Customer, ISP2 can't do anything to share the load with ISP1. This point brings up the other disadvantage, which is lack of reliability. If ISP2 doesn't know about the ISP1 address space being used by Customer, then if the ISP1-Customer link goes down, all the nodes numbered out of ISP1's space become inaccessible. The only way to fix this problem is for Customer to announce the network out of ISP1's space to ISP2 and vice versa. Although this solution might fix the reliability problem, it creates the same problems described for the first and second addressing options involving the longer prefixes being magnets for traffic and the restrictions created by the new, strict routing policies.

The fourth option—having Customer get its own address space from a registry independent of either ISP1 or ISP2—offers some of the most control but does so at the cost of aggregation. Specifically, if Customer has its own address space, there wouldn't be an issue of different parts of the Internet having longer matches than others; instead, the whole Internet would see the same prefix. Again, though, this brings up the issue of the strict routing policies. Unless Customer receives the type of address space that would get through the route filters, Customer might end up having no connectivity at all. Assuming that Customer gets address space that makes it through the route filters, some control is needed over which provider uses which path to reach Customer. For example, if ISP1 is the largest ISP in the picture, Customer may want ISP1 to reach Customer via the ISP1-Customer link but have both ISP2 and ISP3 reach Customer via the ISP2-Customer link. This can be done with **AS-PATH manipulation**, in which the AS-PATH is made artificially longer on the announcement sent from Customer to ISP1. This doesn't affect ISP1's selection because other factors, such as LOCAL-PREF value, will ensure that the ISP1-Customer link is selected. However, the AS-PATH manipulation has an effect on ISP3. If the AS-PATH on the route learned from ISP2 is shorter than the

AS-PATH on the route learned from ISP1, then ISP3 will use ISP2 to reach Customer.

The issues described earlier regarding how a multihomed subscriber does its addressing and how that address space is aggregated, if at all, are the main issues of load sharing from the ISPs to the subscriber. For load sharing in the other direction, the issue is basically the same as for a subscriber multihomed to a single provider. If the areas of topology closest to the points where each ISP connects produce similar amounts of traffic, a closest exit routing policy would produce reasonable load sharing. If this is not the case, other measures must be taken. These other measures end up involving one or more of the ISPs announcing some number of routes so that the subscriber favors one link over the others for reaching various parts of the Internet.

A tangent that should be explored briefly is the importance of addressing within a subscriber's network. Addressing is obviously an important issue in many ways to all networks. But the preceding discussion points out how addressing can be critical to subscribers with respect to its ability to support various types of multihoming. In addition to multihoming, a subscriber's ability to readdress its network without expending tremendous effort gives that subscriber more agility to make changes for internal reasons or to do things such as change ISPs. For these reasons, subscribers should seriously consider using technologies such as DHCP (Dynamic Host Control Protocol) as a way of achieving this added agility.

3.6 A View into Providers' Use of BGP

ISPs, particularly the largest ones, often have very complicated BGP configurations. This section briefly describes some of the BGP-related issues that concern large providers and the approaches that they take in dealing with them.

3.6.1 Aggregation

As discussed in numerous places in this book, aggregation is critical to the survivability of the Internet's routing system. The essence of the Internet is its ability to allow any two users to talk to each other. If the routing system does not scale, this essence will be lost and users will have only partial connectivity. For this reason, it is critical that both providers and subscribers take care to configure their networks so that the maximum possible aggregation is achieved.

Providers do basically two types of aggregation. The first type of aggregation involves a provider only announcing its aggregates to neighboring ASs. This kind of aggregation helps routing between ASs scale well. This type of aggregation is typically achieved by filtering the routes that a provider advertises to its neighbors so that the aggregates are advertised and the more-specifics are filtered and not advertised.

The other type of aggregation is completely internal to a provider's network. Imagine that a large provider has been assigned a /14 prefix for delegating address space to customers. If the provider assigned /24s out of this prefix to customers located at arbitrary locations in the network, the provider could end up carrying 1,024 /24s in its I-BGP mesh; each /24 would be routed separately from every other /24. Instead, what is typically done is to break up the aggregate into subaggregates and assign the subaggregates to access routers. When a subscriber orders a connection to the provider, the provider decides the access router to which the subscriber will connect and delegates address space to that subscriber based on the subaggregate assigned to the access router. If this approach were taken and /19s were assigned to routers, only 32 /19 routing entries would be required.

3.6.2 Filtering Transit Customers

Because of the nature of the relationship between a subscriber and a provider with respect to the routing system, the provider must take great care in managing the associated routing information. Specifically, because a provider readvertises the routes it hears from its transit customers, it must make sure that it doesn't accept *just anything* from those customers. Instead, the provider should apply a filter to the routes that it hears and accept only the routes listed in the filter. Small networks can build these filters manually, often with the help of the customer itself. Larger networks may choose an automated method such as a **routing registry** so that filters can be built off-line and then automatically deployed to access routers on some kind of a schedule.

3.6.3 Public Interconnect Points

There are many books on TCP/IP and the Internet that cover the evolution of the Internet in detail from its origins as a research project through to simultaneous research and military use and finally where we are now, with the Internet as a self-supporting commercial network and service. This book doesn't repeat this history, although it discusses the transition from the research and military stage to the commercial stage, with particular emphasis on the interconnections between networks.

During the research phase starting in the middle 1980s, the U.S. government's National Science Foundation (NSF) funded the infrastructure and operation of the NSFNET. The NSFNET basically served as the backbone of the Internet, connecting military, government, research, and academic institutions as well as other networks that provided connectivity to such organizations. The transition from the research to the commercial phase happened through the end of 1994 and beginning of 1995.

Starting with the decommissioning of the NSFNET in late 1994 and early 1995, there was no longer a single backbone for the Internet. Instead, multiple companies provided this function. At the time, the main providers were ANS, MCI, and Sprint. For full connectivity to be maintained, the idea of a public interconnect point or exchange point was developed. (Actually, this idea had existed even during the time of the NSFNET because some of the providers were commercial in nature, and the NSF's policy prevented commercial traffic from consuming resources on the NSFNET. Early commercial providers established exchanges such as the Metropolitan Area Exchanges [MAEs] and Commercial Internet Exchange [CIX] to connect to each other without having to go through the NSFNET.) These interconnect points typically involve some kind of layer 2 infrastructure such as an Ethernet, a FDDI ring, or an ATM switch. Various providers buy point-to-point circuits from their networks to the location of the interconnect point and connect that circuit to a router at the interconnect that the provider owns. Each provider decides which other providers it wants to exchange traffic with at the interconnect and configures E-BGP sessions. The result is that dynamic routing information and subsequent user

These interconnect points can provide an economical way for networks to connect to one another without having to procure a large number of point-to-point links. However, they also create their own set of unique issues. First, there is only one point-to-point link from a provider's network to the interconnect point, but there are many peers at the interconnect point, and that makes it difficult to control the amount of traffic that each provider sends. The other major problem encountered is dishonest use of a provider's network. Specifically, imagine that ISP1, ISP2, and ISP3 are all at the same interconnect point. Further imagine that ISP1 agreed to peer with ISP2 but not ISP3. Theoretically, this means that ISP1 does not want to receive any traffic from ISP3. However, experience has shown that a number of unscrupulous ISPs configure their routers with either specific or default routes pointing toward other ISPs on an interconnect point. So, in this example, ISP3 might configure a specific or a default route pointing toward ISP1. This is in clear violation of ISP1's policy with respect to ISP3, but routers at the time didn't have the ability to filter out this traffic.

The solution to both problems (rate-controlling individual ISPs and illegal use of a provider's network) was to come up with new features for the interfaces connecting to the layer 2 infrastructures. One feature was to be able to explicitly permit or deny traffic coming into an interface from a certain layer 2 address. The other feature allowed a permitted source to control the rate at which that source could send to the interface.

4

BGP Extensions

The Internet has seen many protocols come and go. Experience has shown that needs change over time, primarily because of growth, and protocols must change to accommodate them. For example, a routing protocol that works in a 100-node network might fail miserably in a 1,000,000-node network. This observation isn't limited to routing protocols. For example, most current mechanisms used for congestion control in TCP (for example, slow start and congestion avoidance) were not part of the original specification. Instead, these mechanisms were developed to remedy unanticipated failure situations.

The point is that the Internet has established a pattern of requiring more and more from its protocols. Sometimes these new requirements can be met with changes to a protocol's implementation. For example, most of the congestion-control mechanisms in TCP have nothing to do with the format of data transmitted and instead reflect the way a host controls its sending rate and volume based on detected packet loss. As a result, these changes could be incorporated into implementations without requiring changes to the specification. In other cases new requirements necessitate modest changes to the protocol. Sometimes the existing version of the protocol can be extended to meet the new requirements. A recent addition to TCP is the **SACK (selective acknowledgment)** feature. Because the original TCP specification allowed options to be added over time, SACK could be added to TCP without having to create a new version of TCP. At other times, a new version of the protocol might be required. For example, the standardization of CIDR by the IETF required a new EGP because BGP3 intrinsically could not support it. Finally, in instances when a fundamental change is needed to meet a set of requirements, a whole new protocol is created. The evolution of inter-domain routing in the Internet has produced protocols such as HELLO, GGP, EGP, and now BGP.

We can learn at least two lessons from these experiences with respect to designing protocols for the Internet. The first is that, because the Internet is an almost organic thing that can change dramatically over time, some protocols die a natural death; the designer should accept this, learn from the change, and go on to design a new protocol that meets the new set of requirements. The second lesson is that the design of a protocol should not be hard-wired to a set of demands at any particular point in time, or it will surely become limiting.

The current version of BGP is a good example of a protocol that has adapted to changing requirements since its initial deployment in the summer of 1993. This chapter discusses some of the major extensions that have been made to BGP since its original specification. In addition to describing the details of the additions, this chapter explains the needs that motivated the additions.

4.1 Internal BGP Scaling

The purpose of the first set of extensions made to BGP was to improve the scaling ability of I-BGP. Remember that the BGP specification indicates that a BGP speaker cannot advertise a route to an I-BGP neighbor if that BGP speaker originally heard the route from another I-BGP speaker. One of the results was a requirement for a full mesh of I-BGP sessions within an AS. Figure 4-1 shows a full mesh of I-BGP sessions in an AS with eight routers.

This repetitive diagram demonstrates how extreme full meshes are. In this case there are eight routers in the AS, each of which peers with seven other routers, for a result of 28 I-BGP sessions within the AS ((8*7)/2). If a ninth router were added to the mesh, the number of I-BGP sessions would become 36. A tenth router would raise it to 45. Figure 4-2 shows a projection of the number of I-BGP sessions required for ASs with as many as 50 routers.

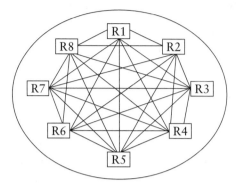

Figure 4-1 *Full mesh of I-BGP sessions*

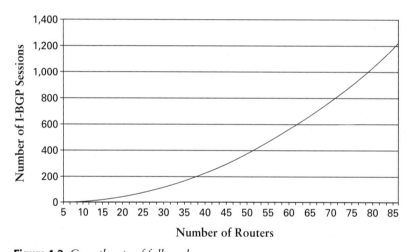

Figure 4-2 *Growth rate of full meshes*

The point is that full meshes scale very poorly. Of the resources that are depleted in a way that is fundamentally not scalable, the CPU on the router is the main one, although memory and bandwidth are also used very inefficiently.

When BGP was first deployed, the number of routers in ASs was low enough that a full mesh of I-BGP sessions could be supported.

However, the Internet was growing at a rapid pace before BGP was deployed, and that growth rate continued after BGP was deployed. The ASs that made up the Internet also grew. In particular, the large ISPs had plans to expand their networks so that a full mesh of I-BGP sessions would not have been supportable by commercially available routers at the time. As a result, extensions were made to the protocol that relaxed the full mesh requirement but ensured that all routers within the AS continued to know about all routes. Two approaches were used to solve the problem; both of them are still in use. These approaches make I-BGP more scalable, so neither one is inherently better. The next two sections describe these two approaches.

4.1.1 Route Reflection

The first approach to solving the problem of full meshes for I-BGP is called **route reflection**. The idea behind route reflection is to add hierarchy to I-BGP. In this way, some routers selectively readvertise routes between routers within the same AS so that all routers within the AS know about all routes but do so without a full mesh.

Route reflection introduces the terms **route reflector** and **route reflector client**. A route reflector is a router whose BGP implementation supports the readvertisement of routes between I-BGP neighbors. A route reflector client is a router that depends on a route reflector to readvertise its routes to the entire AS, and also depends on that route reflector to learn about routes from the rest of the network. Note that a route reflector client doesn't do anything differently than what is called for in the original BGP specification, and it doesn't require any special configuration to interface with a route reflector. Figure 4-3 shows an example AS that uses route reflection.

In this figure we see that AS1 has four route reflector clients (RR-C1, RR-C2, RR-C3, and RR-C4) and three route reflectors (RR1, RR2, and RR3). RR-C1 and RR-C2 each has an I-BGP session with RR1. RR-C3 and RR-C4 each has an I-BGP session with RR2. RR1, RR2, and RR3 have I-BGP sessions with each other. We also see one router in AS2 (E-BGP Neighbor) and an E-BGP session between that router and RR-C2. E-BGP Neighbor advertises a route for 138.39.0.0/16 to RR-C2 via E-BGP. In a nutshell, route reflection provides the ability for the route 138.39.0.0/16 that RR-C2 hears via E-BGP to be advertised to all routers in AS1 with only the seven I-BGP sessions shown in

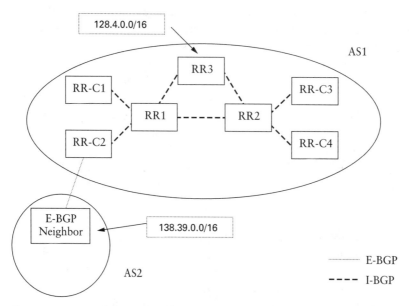

Figure 4-3 *Example I-BGP mesh with route reflection*

Figure 4-3 rather than the 21 sessions that would be required with a full mesh.

In this example RR-C2 will advertise **138.39.0.0/16** to RR1 as usual. RR1 is configured to be a route reflector for RR-C2. Said another way, RR-C2 is a client of RR1. Because of this configuration, when RR1 receives the route from RR-C2, RR1 will readvertise that route to all its I-BGP neighbors. Specifically, RR1 will advertise the route to RR-C1, RR2, and RR3. So part of the role of a route reflector is to readvertise routes learned from a route reflector client further into the I-BGP mesh. The other part of route reflection is to ensure that a route reflector client hears all the routes from the rest of the AS. This part can be demonstrated by explaining what RR2 does when it receives the route for **138.39.0.0/16** from RR1. Because RR2 is the reflector for RR-C3 and RR-C4, when RR2 receives routes from other I-BGP speakers, it must readvertise those routes to RR-C3 and RR-C4. In this example when RR2 receives the route for **138.39.0.0/16**, it will readvertise that route to RR-C3 and RR-C4. As a result, the entire AS knows about the route for 138.39.0.0/16 without needing a full mesh of I-BGP sessions.

Note carefully that route reflectors don't readvertise routes between nonclients. For example, referencing Figure 4-3 again, imagine that RR3 advertises a route for 128.4.0.0/16 to RR1 and RR2. For the route reflector clients to have complete knowledge of routes, RR1 will re-advertise that route to RR-C1 and RR-C2, and in addition RR2 will readvertise the route to RR-C3 and RR-C4. However, the important distinction is that RR1 will not readvertise the route to RR2 nor vice versa. Route reflection does not change the behavior for readvertise-ment between nonclients—route reflectors do not readvertise routes between nonclients.

An important point about route reflection involves the NEXT-HOP attribute. It is important that route reflection work transparently. Specifically, the flow of traffic must continue to be controlled by the IGP's route to the NEXT-HOP attribute (the loopback address of the router that injected the route into the I-BGP mesh) and not by the topology of the I-BGP reflection hierarchy. To meet this requirement, the NEXT-HOP attribute must be preserved throughout the I-BGP mesh. So when a route reflector reflects routes between peering ses-sions, the router must preserve the NEXT-HOP attribute.

The extensions made to the BGP protocol itself to support route reflection were minimal. The major change was to relax the restriction that prevented a router from advertising a route to an I-BGP neighbor that the router heard from another I-BGP neighbor. This relaxation made it possible for routing announcements within an AS to loop. To prevent this, the extensions made for route reflection included two new attributes.

The first new attribute introduced for route reflection is the ORIGINATOR-ID attribute. The attribute type code for this new attribute is 9, and the attribute is optional and nontransitive. The length of the attribute is always four octets. The ORIGINATOR-ID attribute is used to record the router ID of the router that originated the route into the I-BGP mesh. When a route reflector learns a route from one of its clients, it adds the ORIGINATOR-ID attribute to the route and sets the value to be the router ID of the client. A route reflector can check the value of this attribute before reflecting a route to a router. A route reflector never advertises a route to a router if that router's router ID is listed in the ORIGINATOR-ID attribute. As an example, referencing Figure 4-3, if RR1 learns a route from RR-C1 and advertises that route onto RR2 and RR3, RR1 will add an ORIGINATOR-ID attribute with RR-C1's router ID. If for some reason RR1 learns that same route again, the presence of the ORIGINATOR-ID attribute will ensure that RR1 does not readvertise the route back to RR-C1.

The second new attribute introduced for route reflection is the CLUSTER-LIST attribute. The attribute type code for this new attribute is 10, and the attribute is optional and nontransitive. The length of the attribute is variable but is a multiple of four octets. The CLUSTER-LIST attribute is used to record the path that a route has taken through the route reflection hierarchy. A **cluster** is a route reflector and its clients. Referencing Figure 4-3, RR1, RR-C1, and RR-C2 make up one cluster; RR2, RR-C3, and RR-C4 make up another cluster. When a route reflector advertises a route to a nonclient peer, that route reflector will append the current cluster ID to the CLUSTER-LIST attribute (creating the attribute for the first time if necessary). When a route reflector learns a route from a nonclient, the route reflector checks the CLUSTER-LIST attribute and rejects the route if it detects that the route has already visited the cluster in which the route reflector is located. When there is only one route reflector in a cluster (as in the preceding example), the cluster ID is the router ID of the route reflector. For clusters that have more than one route reflector, the cluster ID is a configured four-octet value.

4.1.2 AS Confederations

The second approach taken to solve the problem of scaling with full meshes of I-BGP sessions is **AS confederations**. Whereas the fundamental characteristic of route reflection that helps I-BGP scaling is hierarchy, AS confederations use divide-and-conquer. Both techniques have a long history of use, both in networking and in computer science in general, to improve protocols, algorithms, and so on. The basic approach of AS confederations is shown in Figure 4-4.

At the highest level, an AS confederation takes what used to be a single AS and splits it into many sub-ASs. For example, in the diagram we see that AS1 has been split into ASs 10, 11, 12, 13, and 14. From the perspective of ASs outside the confederation, the original AS doesn't

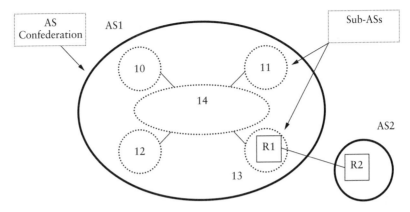

Figure 4-4 *An AS confederation*

look any different. For example, R2 in AS2 cannot see ASs 10 through 14 and instead sees everything as AS1.

The described behavior implies that, within the confederation, special steps are taken. Specifically, a router within a confederation is configured with two things: the ASN for the confederation itself (AS1 in this case) and all the members of the confederation (ASs 10 through 14 in this case).

There is a regular full mesh of I-BGP sessions within a sub-AS, and nothing is special about them.

BGP sessions between routers in two different sub-ASs of the same confederation (sometimes called EIBGP sessions) are like regular E-BGP but with some changes. First, whereas in regular E-BGP if a route is learned that contains the LOCAL-PREF attribute, that attribute must be ignored. For EIBGP sessions, this is allowed. Imagine a route advertised by R2 in AS2 to R1 in sub-AS13. R1 will have policy configuration that establishes a LOCAL-PREF value for that route within all of AS1. Because this value must be known throughout all of AS1, sub-AS13 must be allowed to advertise it into sub-AS14, and from there sub-AS14 must be allowed to advertise the LOCAL-PREF to the other sub-ASs. As with allowing the LOCAL-PREF attribute to traverse sub-AS boundaries, an AS confederation allows the NEXT-HOP to traverse sub-AS boundaries without being changed. This implies something fundamental about AS confederations: it assumes that a single IGP runs across the entire confederation. For this reason, it only makes sense to allow the NEXT-HOP attribute to be set by the first-hop router in the confederation and have that value stay on the route inside all the confederation. The third difference between E-BGP and EIBGP is that, because we want to prevent looping routing announcements within the confederation, new path segment types are introduced for the AS-PATH attribute. AS-CONFED-SET (path segment type 3) and AS-CONFED-SEQUENCE (path segment type 4) are used similarly to AS-SET and AS-SEQUENCE except that the new attributes are used only within a confederation. For example, if R1 learned a route from R2 and advertises that route via EIBGP to a router in sub-AS14, R1 will add an AS-CONFED-SEQUENCE to the AS-PATH attribute and include AS13 in that new path segment. When routers within sub-AS14 readvertise the route to the other sub-ASs in the confederation, they will prepend AS14 to the AS-CONFED-SEQUENCE.

An E-BGP session between a router in a sub-AS of a confederation and a router outside the confederation is the place where the structure within the confederation is hidden. Consider what happens when R1, which is in the confederation, advertises a route to R2, which is not in the confederation. In doing this, R1 strips any AS-CONFED-SEQUENCE and/or AS-CONFED-SET path segments from the AS-PATH attribute and adds AS1 to the AS-PATH attribute in the usual manner. Specifically, R1 will prepend AS1 to the existing AS-PATH attribute or add a new AS-PATH attribute containing AS1.

4.2 Route Flap Dampening

Imagine an AS that has a single connection to its upstream provider. Now imagine that the link is having a problem so that it is constantly going up and down. In this situation when the link goes down, taking the BGP session with it, the upstream provider will withdraw the routes from all its neighbors and so on. When the link comes back up and the BGP session is established and routes are exchanged, those routes will again be advertised globally. When the circuit problem manifests itself again, the routes will again be withdrawn. This behavior can continue until the underlying problem is fixed. This kind of behavior isn't terrible in a localized area, but in the Internet's global routing mesh, this amount of flux in routing state is worrisome. This behavior is called **route flapping**. When a specific prefix is withdrawn and then advertised again, that process is considered an individual route flap.

An extension to BGP has been proposed to allow these route flaps to be **dampen**ed. This extension **suppress**es the advertisement of the route somewhere close to the source until the route becomes stable. As of this writing, the route flap dampening proposal is in draft form. The specification is complex, so some details might change. The description that follows is much more simplified than the specification, although it should provide enough of a conceptual description to help you understand the feature. Note that even though this extension is in draft form with respect to the standards process, the feature is supported by a number of router vendors and used by most large ISPs.

Before we explain the details of route flap dampening, it should be noted that aggregation often masks flapping. Consider Figure 4-5. In this figure we see Customer, which receives transit service from ISP1; E-BGP is used for dynamic routing between them. Customer uses the prefix **138.39.1/24**, which is a more-specific of ISP1's aggregate **138.39/16**. ISP1 and ISP2 connect to each other. Because ISP1 treats **138.39/16** as an aggregate, it will not advertise the more-specific to ISP2. Instead, it will announce only the /**16**. In this situation if the link between Customer and ISP1 were to constantly go up and down, ISP2 would not see any route flaps.

However, aggregation does not obviate route flap dampening. This is true for at least two reasons. First, the reality is that many sites are

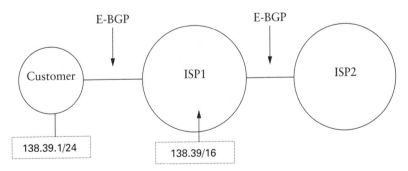

Figure 4-5 *Dampening example*

numbered using legacy addresses that cannot be aggregated. This problem could be solved by having all the sites renumber into prefixes that are aggregatable—a laudable but unlikely goal. The second, more fundamental reason that aggregation cannot take the place of route flap dampening is that even a highly aggregated route can flap (for example, a very large ISP running routing software with a bug causing constant crashes and reboots will flap all its routes to its neighbors).

Route flap dampening is not an extension to the protocol per se. It is analogous to policy in this way. Specifically, routing policy has nothing to do with how BGP messages appear on the wire or the mandated ways in which some routes are selected over others. Instead, routing policy simply represents a given BGP speaker's ability to accept or reject a route heard from a neighbor. Similarly, route flap dampening allows a BGP speaker to take into account the past stability of a route in deciding whether to use or readvertise that route.

Route flap dampening works by storing a **penalty** value with each route. The penalty for a route is increased by a certain amount if the route flaps and is decremented over time at a particular rate. If the penalty for a route reaches a particular value, the route will be suppressed, meaning that it will not be a candidate for a forwarding entry on the local system nor will it be readvertised to peers. The route will stay suppressed until the penalty falls below a certain threshold (remember that the penalty value is decremented over time).

Note that one of the ramifications of route flap dampening from an implementation perspective is that when, for example, BGP speaker R1 withdraws a route from R2, R2 cannot completely forget about that route. Instead, R2 must store data about the route, even after it is withdrawn, so that the associated penalty is not lost.

A few other notes should be made about route flap dampening. The first concerns how the extension relates to I-BGP versus E-BGP. This extension is for E-BGP and not I-BGP. The main reason for not dampening in I-BGP is the risk of inconsistent routing within an AS or forwarding loops. Consider Figure 4-6.

In this figure we see that AS1 has three routers: R1, R2, and R3. R1 is physically connected to R2, and R2 is physically connected to R3. They share a full mesh of I-BGP connections. Now imagine that these I-BGP sessions were subject to dampening but they didn't have identical configurations with respect to the penalties applied, the suppress threshold, and/or the unsuppress threshold. A route that R1 injects

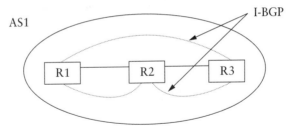

Figure 4-6 *I-BGP and dampening*

into the I-BGP mesh is suppressed by R2 but not by R3. Because R3 isn't suppressing it, R3 is free to readvertise the route to other ASs. If one of those other ASs forwards traffic for the prefix to R3, R3 will forward it to R2 because that is the physical path R3 takes to reach R1. Unfortunately, if R2 is suppressing the route, R2 will not have a forwarding entry. The result is that AS1 becomes a black hole for the prefix because it advertises the route in BGP but does not correctly deliver the traffic. In another failure scenario R2 has a forwarding entry for an aggregate that includes the suppressed prefix. If that forwarding entry points to the link from R2 to R3, a forwarding loop between R3 and R2 results.

The final note has to do with how some people have configured the values in practice. An implementation of dampening can take a number of things into account for incrementing and decrementing penalties and deciding what the suppress and unsuppress thresholds should be. One of these factors is the length of the prefix. For example, an ISP may decide that it wants to dampen longer prefixes more aggressively than shorter prefixes. Some ISPs have used this as a way to encourage people to renumber into address space that is aggregatable by their provider. Subscribers numbered out of addresses that are aggregated by their provider are less likely to be dampened.

4.3 BGP Communities

The BGP **community** is an attribute that was added to BGP to simplify the configuration of complex routing policies. Before we delve into low-level protocol and mechanical details about the community attribute, let's look at a very short conceptual introduction.

At a high level, the capability offered by the community attribute is the ability to associate an identifier with a route. This ability can be useful because a set of routes that are supposed to receive the same treatment with respect to policy can be assigned the same identifier. Imagine that ISP1, ISP2, and ISP3 are all nontransit peers of one another. To enforce the appropriate transit/nontransit relationships, ISP1 will not announce ISP2's routes to ISP3 or vice versa. If ISP1 uses the community attribute to tag the routes learned from ISP2 and ISP3 as having been learned from a nontransit peer, policy at other edges of the network could use the community attribute to decide how to treat the routes.

To understand in more detail the practical usefulness of the community attribute, it is necessary to understand the way that ASs configured things before the attribute was introduced. Consider the example in Figure 4-7.

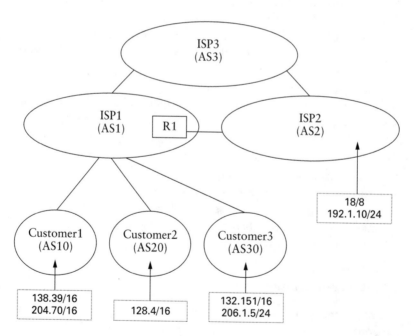

Figure 4-7 *BGP communities example*

In this diagram we see ISP1, ISP2, and ISP3 (ASs 1, 2, and 3, respectively) connecting to one another via physical links and corresponding E-BGP sessions. Customer1, Customer2, and Customer3 (ASs 10, 20, and 30, respectively) are all transit customers of ISP1, and they all speak BGP with ISP1. The prefixes used by each of the customers are shown. Consider what AS1 must do to enforce a routing policy of offering transit service to ASs 10, 20, and 30 but nontransit to AS2 and AS3. On the E-BGP session between R1 in AS1 and some router in AS2, ISP1 must advertise routes only for the prefixes used by its customers, and it must not advertise routes to AS3. Providers initially took two approaches to this configuration. The first approach was to configure R1 with a list of all the prefixes used by ISP1's customers and to use that list to filter routing updates going from R1 into AS2. This example would not be very difficult because only five prefixes are involved. However, in practice even small providers might have several hundreds of prefixes to announce and large providers might have several thousand. If this were a one-time necessity, the complexity of such configurations might be manageable. However, the configuration must change over time—for example, when a new customer gets connected, an old one leaves, or an existing one starts routing a new prefix. The second approach taken involved configuring, for example, R1 with a list of all the ASs used by ISP1's customers. This approach scaled much better than the approach dealing with individual prefixes. However, it shares the same disadvantage of requiring configuration changes every time customers and prefixes come and go. Note also that this configuration must be replicated on every router speaking BGP with another AS. Theoretically, this could mean every router in the AS.

As stated earlier, at a very high level, the feature that BGP communities provides is to identify a route as belonging to a particular *category* (for example, a route that receives transit service versus a route that does not). This categorization of routes is sometimes called **route coloring**. Although it is possible to use this feature in any number of ways, all uses to date have been to place routes in one or more categories, in which all routes in a particular category are manipulated in the same way with respect to routing policy. There are a few well-known communities that have standardized behaviors. The remaining values are used within an individual AS or between a set of two or more ASs in any way they decide. For these local-use communities, the primary application is to simplify the configuration of routing policy by identifying which routes are transit and which are not, but the feature is actually very general and can be used in a number of ways, one of which will be described here.

4.3.1 Protocol Details of the Community Attribute

The BGP community attribute is optional and nontransitive and is type code 8. The attribute is a list of individual community values, each of which is a four-octet value, so the Attribute Length field is always an integer multiple of four. A route can potentially be associated with many BGP communities, so there is no limit on field length (except for maximum length of the packet carrying the BGP UPDATE message). A community is identified by a four-octet value, and a route is considered a member of that community if the UPDATE message for the route contains a community attribute that includes that value.

The community values 0x00000000 through 0x0000FFFF are reserved, as are 0xFFFF0000 through 0xFFFFFFFF. To help avoid conflict in community values, the high-order two octets conventionally contain an ASN. The low-order two octets are chosen by the AS identified by the high-order two octets. For example, if AS200 decides to use the value 666 in the low-order two octets to identify nontransit routes, the whole four-octet value would be 0x000C8029A (decimal 13107866). For simplicity in entering and reading community values formatted this way, implementations of BGP accept and display community values formatted as 200:666, in which the colon separates the ASN and the low-order two octets. If AS500 happened to pick the low-order two-octet value of 666 for a different purpose, there would be no conflict between the two four-octet values.

4.3.2 Example Use of the Community Attribute: Enforcing Transit Policy

Let's reconsider Figure 4-7. BGP communities could be used as follows to ease the configuration that enforces the appropriate transit versus nontransit policy.

1. The E-BGP sessions between AS1 and AS10, AS20, and AS30 are configured to add BGP community 1:777 to routes learned via those E-BGP sessions. So the community value 1:777 is

used to identify routes that should receive transit service. If a BGP community attribute is associated with a route learned, a new attribute can simply be added to the list. If no community attribute is present, one can be added with only the community 1:777 in the list.

2. The E-BGP sessions between AS1 and AS2 and AS3 are configured to add BGP community 1:666 to routes learned via those E-BGP sessions. So the community value 1:666 is used to identify routes that should not receive transit service.

3. The E-BGP sessions between AS1 and AS2 and AS3 are configured to filter the routes advertised to AS2 and AS3. Specifically, AS1 will advertise only routes to AS2 and AS3 that are members of the 1:777 community, and it will not advertise routes in the 1:666 community.

4. Finally, the E-BGP sessions between AS1 and AS10, AS20, and AS30 are configured to send whatever the customers have requested (full routes, default only, and so on).

The main advantage of this scheme is that it implements exactly the right routing policy but does so without requiring the routers peering with nontransit ASs to be updated as customers and prefixes come and go.

4.3.3 Well-Known Community Values

As mentioned earlier, in addition to the local-use community values, there are well-known community values. The three values standardized in the original specification of the BGP community attribute were NO-EXPORT (0xFFFFFF01), NO-ADVERTISE (0xFFFFFF02), and NO-EXPORT-SUBCONFED (0xFFFFFF03). Each of these values will be explained in turn.

If a BGP speaker receives a route with a NO-EXPORT community listed in the community attribute, then that BGP speaker must not export that route beyond the local AS. Consider Figure 4-8.

In this diagram we see AS1 and AS2 connected to each other in two places. We also see AS2 and AS3 connected to each other in one place. Finally, we see that AS1 uses the prefix 138.39/16. As discussed in Section 3.5, it may be necessary for AS1 to announce more granular routing information to AS2 than just the /16 in order for load sharing to be

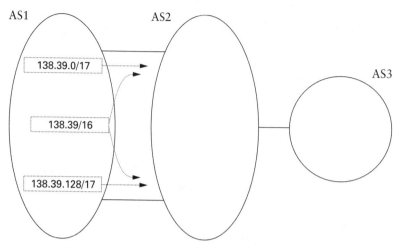

Figure 4-8 *Example use of NO-EXPORT*

effective. Let's assume that AS1 advertises both the /16 and the two /17s
that are more specific to that /16, where each /17 is preferred over one
of the links. Assuming that the amount of traffic going to the two
halves of the /16 is about equal, this routing policy should result in
fairly good load sharing between the two links. If these announcements
of more-specifics are required, however, there is a risk that AS2 will
readvertise the /17s to AS3. This would result in AS3 seeing more
routes than necessary without deriving any benefit from it. So it is
strongly preferred that AS2 not advertise the two /17s to AS3. Without
BGP communities, special configuration would have to be put on the
router in AS2 that peers with AS3 so that those two /17s are not advertised. This approach complicates the configuration process because it
would require changes for each new similarly multihomed customer
that AS2 gets. Instead, AS1 can attach the community NO-EXPORT
to the two /17s as it advertises them to AS2. As a result, AS2 will carry
both the /16 and the two /17s in its I-BGP mesh. The /17s will be used
for forwarding, because they are longer matches than the one /16, so
traffic will be forwarded to support the multihoming policy. However,
when AS2 peers with AS3, it will advertise only the one /16 and neither
of the two /17s, thus keeping aggregation optimal.

The NO-EXPORT-SUBCONFED community is similar to NO-EXPORT except that the former is used in AS confederation situations. Specifically, NO-EXPORT-SUBCONFED is used if a network administrator doesn't want a route advertised beyond a sub-AS of a confederation. If NO-EXPORT were used in this situation, the route would be advertised to all sub-ASs within the confederation.

The NO-ADVERTISE community is somewhat similar in that it restricts readvertisement of a route but does so over a narrower scope. Specifically, if a BGP speaker learns a route with the NO-ADVERTISE community, that BGP speaker must not readvertise that route beyond the local router. Consider Figure 4-9.

In this diagram we see routers R1, R2, and R3 all on the same FDDI LAN. R1 is in AS1, and R2 and R3 are in AS2. R1 and R2 have an E-BGP session between them. R3 doesn't speak BGP. Finally, we see that AS2 uses the prefix **138.39/16** and almost that entire prefix is used by topology behind R2. The exception is **138.39.1/24**, which is connected to R3. AS2 would like the forwarding of packets destined for the **138.39.1/24** prefix to be optimal, and that means that it would like R1 to forward packets directly to R3 instead of forwarding those packets to R2, thus forcing R2 to send those packets back onto the FDDI to

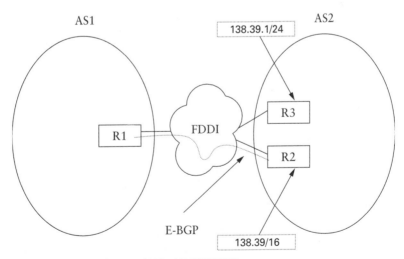

Figure 4-9 *Example use of NO-ADVERTISE*

R3. This use is perfect for the third-party NEXT-HOP feature, in which R2 advertises a route for 138.39.1/24 to R1 but specifies R3's FDDI interface address as the NEXT-HOP. To ensure that the rest of the 138.39/16 prefix is routed correctly, R2 must advertise a second route for 138.39/16 with itself as the NEXT-HOP. Therein lies the problem: if R2 advertises both of these prefixes to R1, then R1 will faithfully readvertise them into its I-BGP mesh and, if they meet policy, onto neighbor ASs. This is a waste; R1 is the only router that needs to know about the special routing for 138.39.1/24 because the rest of AS1 only needs to know to forward packets destined for 138.39/16 to R1 and then R1 will take responsibility. This use is ideal for the NO-ADVERTISE community. If R2 includes the NO-ADVERTISE community with the route for 138.39.1/24 but not with the route for 138.39/16, R1 will not advertise the /24 to any other router. As a result, forwarding for the two prefixes is optimal but aggregation is not weakened.

4.3.4 Example Use of the Community Attribute: Automatic Backup Routes

The final point about BGP communities concerns another application of general communities (as opposed to well-known communities). Consider Figure 4-10.

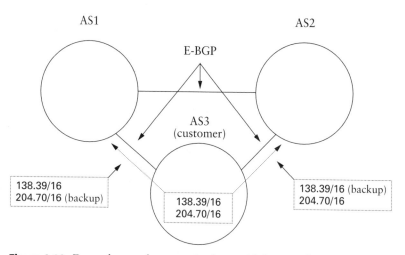

Figure 4-10 *Example use of community for establishing preference*

In this diagram we see that AS1 and AS2 are ISPs and that AS3 is a multihomed customer of both AS1 and AS2. AS3 uses two prefixes: 138.39/16 and 204.70/16. The approach AS3 has chosen to take with multihoming is to use AS1 for traffic coming to 138.39/16 and AS2 for traffic coming to 204.70/16. Because AS3 wants to use the redundancy inherent in multihoming, however, AS3 wants to make sure that if one of the links goes down, the other will take over for both prefixes. To implement this, AS3 would need to announce both prefixes via both E-BGP sessions. If no additional configuration were in place, though, AS1 would use its direct link to AS3 for both prefixes, and AS2 would use its direct link to AS3 for both prefixes. In other words, the desired multihoming policy wouldn't be implemented. The reason is that, in practice, AS1 and AS2 would by default give the routes they learn from customers a higher preference than routes they learn from nontransit peers. The required action is for AS1 to treat the 204.70/16 announcement as backup and to have AS2 treat the 138.39/16 announcement as backup. Note that MULTI-EXIT-DISCRIMINATORs cannot be used here because there are not multiple links between a single pair of ASs. One option is for AS1 to configure its router that peers with AS3 to give the route for 204.70/16 a lower preference than the preference it gives to routes learned from AS2. If AS1 has many customers that are multihomed in this way, it becomes an administrative challenge to do this much configuration work. Additionally, if for some reason AS3 needs to change the preferences assigned, it must make a request to AS1 and wait for a response.

An alternative to this manual configuration is to apply BGP communities in the following way.

1. AS1 configures its router that peers with AS3 to look for routes with the community 1:20 and to react by setting the LOCAL-PREF for the route to 60. (So AS1 has defined the community 1:20 to be a signal for setting the LOCAL-PREF to 60. Note that, in reality, it would make sense for the low-order two octets of the community to be the same as the LOCAL-PREF to ease memorizing the meaning of the community. In this example the values are different, pointing out that it isn't in any way required.) If no such community is present, AS1 reacts in the default way of setting the LOCAL-PREF to 100.

2. Similarly, AS2 configures its router that peers with AS3 to look for routes with the community 2:70 and to react by setting the LOCAL-PREF for the route to 70. If no such community is present, AS2 reacts in the default way of setting the LOCAL-PREF to 100.

3. AS3 configures its router that peers with AS1 to tag the route for 204.70/16 with the community 1:20.

4. AS3 configures its router that peers with AS2 to tag the route for 138.39/16 with the community 2:70.

As a result, the multihoming policy is implemented without AS1 or AS2 having to deploy special configuration. AS3 is allowed to make any changes it wants at any time without requiring support from AS1 or AS2.

4.4 TCP MD5 Authentication

As discussed earlier, a mechanism is included in the base protocol specification of BGP for doing some amount of security. Specifically, the OPEN message can contain an authentication information optional parameter that can indicate how to predict the value of the Marker field in subsequent messages. However, neither the base specification nor a later extension described a specific use for the authentication information optional parameter. The reason is that there is no value in securing only the application-layer BGP session and not the underlying TCP connection. Specifically, if the TCP connection is not secured somehow but the BGP session is, attackers can still attack the underlying TCP connection and disrupt communication. For example, TCP RST (reset) messages can be sent by an attacker, causing the segment numbers used by the two legitimate TCP endpoints to get out of sync; as a result, the BGP session may terminate. For this reason, adding practical security to BGP requires securing at least the TCP connection.

A mechanism for securing TCP connections that support BGP sessions has been proposed and is widely used in practice. A full description of this proposal would require delving into complex details about TCP and cryptography. Rather than present this complexity, this book gives only a high-level description. Readers interested in the details should see the specification of the proposal.

The specific mechanism that has been proposed is an option added to TCP that can hold what is called an **MD5 digest**. MD5 is a cryptographic algorithm that takes as input a message of an arbitrary length and produces as output a 16-byte digest. The algorithm is carefully designed so that it is computationally hard to find two messages that produce the same digest. This proposal is called the TCP MD5 authentication option.

Although the proposal is a generic addition to TCP, in practice it is used only with BGP. Each end of a BGP session secured this way is configured with a shared password. TCP segments generated by each end of the BGP session contain the MD5 authentication option, and the MD5 digest contained in the segments is a function of both the data contained in the TCP segment and the configured password. When a router receives a message containing the MD5 authentication option, it calculates the digest in the same way the sender did. If the digest calculated by the receiver does not match the one sent by the sender, the receiver drops the segment. For attackers to successfully attack a BGP session secured in this way, they would have to guess the TCP segment numbers as well as the shared password. Note that in this proposal the password is never sent on the line.

The TCP MD5 authentication option has some known weaknesses. Curious readers should see the document describing the option and its weaknesses. In spite of these weaknesses, the proposal is likely to become a standard because it is widely deployed.[1]

4.5 Multiprotocol

Although the Internet's primary function is to forward IP packets—currently IPv4 packets—there are parts of the Internet that can forward more than just IPv4. Some parts of the Internet can currently forward IPv6 packets (for example, quasi-production test beds that support both IPv4 and IPv6). In addition, there are parts of the Internet

---

1. The administrative bodies that run the Internet's standards process will likely add a note to the specification indicating that it has known weaknesses but was standardized given its wide use. This kind of information attached to standards is often helpful to implementers.

that can forward completely different protocols such as Novell's IPX, Banyan's VINES, and so on (for example, enterprise networks or ISPs that offer these kinds of value-added services). Because BGP is the Internet's inter-domain routing protocol and because it has a huge installed base, there is an interest in using BGP to do routing of protocols in addition to IPv4. In addition to being useful for routing different versions of IP and different protocols all together, another potential use for a multiprotocol BGP is inter-domain IP multicast routing. Since the use of multicast IP began on an Internet-wide basis in the early to mid-1990s, there has been a crisis of sorts in identifying an inter-domain multicast routing protocol that scales well. Multiprotocol extensions to BGP could allow the protocol to be leveraged for this purpose. (Note, though, that the carriage of the routing updates is only a tiny part of what an inter-domain multicast routing protocol would need to do. The hard part in solving this problem is to come up with the underlying algorithms and modes of operation.)

A proposal for adding a multiprotocol routing feature to BGP is in draft form as of this writing. It is possible that some details may change in the final form of the document, and the proposal may never be standardized, although that possibility seems unlikely.

The multiprotocol extensions are embodied in two new attributes: MP-REACH-NLRI and MP-UNREACH-NLRI. MP-REACH-NLRI is used to advertise multiprotocol routes, and MP-UNREACH-NLRI is used to withdraw them. These two new attributes can be used only after the BGP session comes up. This means that, for protocol reasons—such as the BGP identifier, the fact that it runs on top of TCP/IP, and so on—a BGP speaker using the multiprotocol extensions must have at least one IPv4 address. After the BGP session is up, prefixes can be advertised and withdrawn by sending normal UPDATE messages that include either or both of the multiprotocol attributes.

The attributes are backward-compatible. If R1 and R2 have a BGP session and R1 supports the multiprotocol attributes but R2 does not, they can still exchange IPv4 unicast routes even though they cannot exchange multiprotocol routes.

4.5.1 MP-REACH-NLRI

The MP-REACH-NLRI attribute is type code 14, and it is an optional nontransitive attribute. It is formatted as shown in Figure 4-11.

Address Family Identifier (2 octets)
Subsequent Address Family Identifier (1 octet)
Length of Network Address of Next Hop (1 octet)
Network Address of Next Hop (variable length)
Number of SNPAs (1 octet)
Length of First SNPA (1 octet)
First SNPA (variable length)
Length of Second SNPA (1 octet)
Second SNPA (variable length)
...
Length of Last SNPA (1 octet)
Last SNPA (variable length)
Network Layer Reachability Information (variable length)

Figure 4-11 *Format of MP-REACH-NLRI attribute*

The Address Family Identifier field indicates the protocol that this UPDATE message is carrying. The values for various protocols are taken from RFC 1700 (for example, IPv4 is 1, IPv6 is 2, and IPX is 11). The protocol-specific information is contained in the Network Address of Next Hop field and the NLRI field. In other words, advertising an IPv6 route would require an IPv6 next hop and IPv6 NLRI.

The Subsequent Address Family Identifier field further describes the kind of routing information being carried in the UPDATE message. Sub-AFI zero (0) is reserved. Sub-AFIs 128–255 are reserved for use by vendors. There are currently three uses specified for this field:

- Unicast NLRI (sub-AFI 1)
- Multicast NLRI (sub-AFI 2)
- Both unicast and multicast NLRI (sub-AFI 3)

The Length of Network Address of Next Hop field indicates the length of the network address of the next hop. This value is typically implied by the AFI and sub-AFI.

The Network Address of Next Hop field indicates the network address of the node to which traffic should be forwarded toward the destination(s) being advertised in the NLRI field.

The Number of SNPAs field indicates the number of subnetwork points of attachment that are listed in the attribute. If this value is 0, the next field in the attribute is NLRI. An SNPA is a layer 2 address for the node with the address specified in the Network Address of Next Hop field. This SNPA information is included to ease discovering layer 2 addresses for subnetworks such as ATM, Frame Relay, SMDS, and so on. If two routers—R1 and R2—share a BGP session, they obviously already know how to reach each other at some address, or else the TCP connection over which the BGP session runs could not have been established. Including an SNPA for the next hop could be useful for third-party next hop when the receiver of the attribute doesn't necessarily know the layer 2 address of the next hop. If the next hop has multiple attachments to the subnetwork, each one could be listed in a different SNPA field.

The Length of First SNPA field (and other Length of *nth* SNPA fields) indicates the length of the following SNPA. The length is measured in 4-bit chunks. For example, a 48-bit IEEE 802 address such as Ethernet measured this way would have a length of 12.

The First SNPA field (and other *nth* SNPA fields) identifies an SNPA of the node that has the address contained in the Network Address of Next Hop field. The whole attribute must be octet-aligned, so if the Length of *nth* SNPA field for this SNPA is odd, the final 4 bits of this field are padding.

The Network Layer Reachability Information field contains the list of prefixes being advertised in this attribute. Each prefix in the list is formatted as shown in Figure 4-12.

The Length field indicates the number of bits in the prefix. The Prefix field contains the prefix itself followed by enough bits to make the

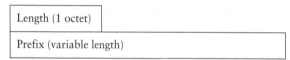

Figure 4-12 *NLRI Field of MP-REACH-NLRI*

length of the whole field be an integer multiple of eight bits. Any trailing bits must be ignored.

When a BGP speaker advertises a multiprotocol route using the MP-REACH-NLRI attribute, the BGP speaker will also use other attributes. For example, the ORIGIN and AS-PATH attributes will always be carried and, for I-BGP, the LOCAL-PREF will always be carried.

The MP-REACH-NLRI attribute allows a BGP speaker to advertise both IPv4 and multiprotocol routes in the same UPDATE message provided that they share the same path attributes. Implementations typically do not do this, however. Instead they typically advertise routes for only one protocol in a single UPDATE. Assuming that only multiprotocol routes are advertised in a given UPDATE message, that message typically contains the MP-REACH-NLRI attribute, the ORIGIN attribute, the AS-PATH attribute, the LOCAL-PREF attribute (if it is an I-BGP session), and other desired attributes such as MULTI-EXIT-DISCRIMINATOR, BGP community, and so on. In an UPDATE message containing only multiprotocol routes the NEXT-HOP attribute will never be included because the MP-REACH-NLRI attribute contains that information. Also, the UPDATE message's standard NLRI field will be empty for UPDATE messages carrying only multiprotocol routes.

4.5.2 MP-UNREACH-NLRI

The MP-UNREACH-NLRI attribute is type code 15 and is an optional nontransitive attribute. It is encoded as shown in Figure 4-13.

The Address Family Identifier and Subsequent Address Family Identifier fields work the same way as in MP-REACH-NLRI to identify the protocol being carried in this attribute.

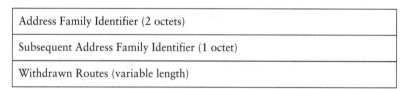

| Address Family Identifier (2 octets) |
| Subsequent Address Family Identifier (1 octet) |
| Withdrawn Routes (variable length) |

Figure 4-13 *Format of MP-UNREACH-NLRI attribute*

The Withdrawn Routes field is the list of prefixes being withdrawn. Each prefix in the list is encoded as shown earlier in Figure 4-12.

The use of the MP-UNREACH-NLRI attribute is semantically identical to the Withdrawn Routes field of the standard UPDATE message. Imagine that router R1 advertises a route for a particular multiprotocol prefix to its BGP neighbor R2 but some time later R1 can no longer reach that prefix. R1 will send an UPDATE message to R2, and that UPDATE message's Path Attributes field will include an MP-UNREACH-NLRI attribute whose Withdrawn Routes field includes the multiprotocol prefix being withdrawn.

4.6 Capabilities Negotiation

It is sometimes useful for a BGP speaker to know the capabilities of a BGP neighbor with respect to protocol extensions such as the multiprotocol attributes. A proposal has been made to add capabilities negotiation to BGP. This proposal is not yet in final form as of this writing, so some details may be different in the final version.

One of the reasons for the capabilities negotiation proposal is the discussion about how to add the multiprotocol feature to BGP. Arguably, it could have been possible to add multiprotocol capabilities to BGP in a simpler and more straightforward way if a new UPDATE message were created. However, it is difficult to add a new UPDATE message in a backward-compatible way. If BGP had the ability to negotiate capabilities, however, it would be possible to use a new type of UPDATE message between peers who support the new message. The multiprotocol feature ended up being achieved without requiring a new UPDATE message. However, the multiprotocol feature could make use of capabilities negotiation to discover the protocols that a neighbor supports.

Capabilities negotiation is achieved with the addition of a new optional parameter called Capabilities. This optional parameter is included in the Optional Parameters field of an OPEN message. Remember that optional parameters are encoded as shown in Figure 4-14.

The Capabilities optional parameter is parameter type 2. The Parameter Length field specifies the length of the Parameter Value field. The

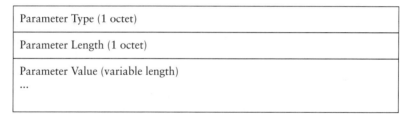

Figure 4-14 *Encoding of OPEN message's Optional Parameters field*

Parameter Value field for Capabilities contains a list of capabilities, each of which is encoded as shown in Figure 4-15.

The Capability Code field identifies the capability supported by the sender of the OPEN message. If the high-order bit of this field is set to 1, the capability is considered *required;* otherwise, the capability is not required. If a BGP speaker that supports capabilities negotiation receives a required capability that it does not support, the BGP speaker should respond with a NOTIFICATION with an error code of OPEN Message Error (error code 2) and a new error subcode. The new OPEN message error subcode is Unsupported Capability, and the error subcode is 7. The Data field of the NOTIFICATION field contains the list of required capabilities that the sender of the NOTIFICATION message does not support, encoded exactly as they were encoded in the Capabilities optional parameter in the OPEN message.

The Capability Length field indicates the length in octets of the Capability Value field.

The Capability Value field contains information specific to the capability code.

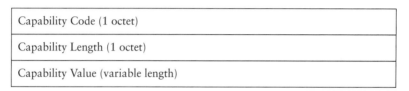

Figure 4-15 *Encoding of Capability item*

Imagine that BGP speaker R1 sends an OPEN message to R2 specifying some number of capabilities as required, and receives a NOTIFICATION message in response indicating that one or more of those capabilities are not supported by R2. R1 should react by attempting to open the BGP session again by sending an OPEN message, but this time listing in the Capabilities optional parameter only the required capabilities that both R1 and R2 support.

Only one use has been specified for the Capabilities optional parameter, and it is in support of the multiprotocol extensions. The capability code for multiprotocol extensions is 1. The capability length is always 4. The encoding of capability value is as shown in Figure 4-16.

The Address Family Identifier field identifies a protocol supported by the sender of the OPEN message using the same values from RFC 1700 as the MP-REACH-NLRI attribute. The next octet is reserved and should be set to zero on transmit and ignored on receipt. The Sub-AFI field identifies a sub-AFI value supported for the AFI. If a BGP speaker supports multiple protocols, the BGP speaker should include multiple occurrences of the multiprotocol extensions capability so that every supported protocol is listed.

Address Family Identifier (2 octets)	Reserved (1 octet)	Sub-AFI (1 octet)

Figure 4-16 *Encoding of capability value for multiprotocol extensions capability*

Appendix A
Resources

This appendix contains a list of references along with an abbreviated description of the reference contents. Most references are documents that are part of the Internet standards process, although there are also some books.

A.1 Internet Standards Process and Documents

Because many references are made to documents that are part of the Internet standards process, we spend a little time describing that standards process. The primary body that produces materials that become Internet standards is the IETF (Internet Engineering Task Force). The IETF can be found on the Web at www.ietf.org. The IETF is currently organized into seven functional areas: Applications, Internet, Operations and Management, Routing, Security, Transport, and User Services. Each area has one or two area directors. All the area directors together form the IESG (Internet Engineering Steering Group). It is the IESG that decides whether and when something becomes a standard. Within each of these areas are a number of working groups. For example, the IDR (inter-domain routing) group is responsible for BGP, and it is in the Routing area. Each working group has one or more chairs who are responsible for running all aspects of the working group according to guidelines created by the IESG and others. Often, there are separate document editors who are responsible for documenting all or part of the work done by the working group.

Documents are an important part of any standards process, and the Internet has no shortage of types and classifications of documents. While a protocol is being designed and developed, draft versions of the associated documents must be published. At this stage, the type of document used is an **Internet-Draft**. Internet-Drafts are named in a way that describes the author and the subject. For example, draft-ietf-idr-bgp4-07.txt is the seventh revision of the Internet-Draft on BGP4 written by the IETF's IDR Working Group. An Internet-Draft may go through many different versions, and the latest version is always made available publicly and for free. Internet-Drafts are works in progress and can be deleted if they haven't been updated for six months. With each revision, an Internet-Draft gets closer to being published as a document that will not expire. This eternal document is called an RFC (Request for Comment). RFCs are numbered sequentially and, once published, are never revised. For example, the most recent publication of the BGP specification is RFC 1771. Note very carefully that an RFC isn't necessarily a standard. RFCs come in several categories: standards track, BCP (Best Current Practice), Informational, Experimental, and Historical. An RFC that is on the standards track is further divided by the stage at which it is located in the standards process. The three stages are, in order, Proposed Standard, Draft Standard, and Standard. As a protocol gathers operational experience and wider acceptance, it is advanced along the standards track. The length of time that a protocol can remain at the Proposed and Draft stages is limited. If a protocol makes it to the Standard stage, it can remain there forever or until it is deprecated to Historical status.

In addition to the IETF's Web site, Internet-Drafts can be retrieved via FTP from the /internet-drafts directory on the following sites:
- ftp.is.co.za (Africa)
- ftp.nordu.net (Europe/North)
- ftp.nis.garr.it (Europe/South)
- munnari.oz.au (Pacific Rim)
- ftp.ietf.org (U.S. East Coast)
- ftp.isi.edu (U.S. West Coast)

When Internet-Drafts are referenced in this appendix, they are referenced without the version number (for example, draft-ietf-idr-bgp4). In this way, you can find the most up-to-date version of the document. Note carefully that Internet-Drafts are temporary documents and are eventually published as RFCs or are abandoned as work items. If an Internet-Draft has been published as an RFC or deleted, the repositories place that information into the filename of the latest version of the document.

Information about RFCs, including the RFCs themselves, can be found on the Web at www.rfc-editor.org. RFCs can also be retrieved from the /in-notes directory on ftp.isi.edu as filenames rfc*NNNN*.txt, where *NNNN* is the number of the RFC (for example, rfc791.txt or rfc2300.txt).

A.2 TCP/IP

All the references listed in this section give more-detailed information about core TCP/IP in general. It is difficult to separate what is core TCP/IP from what isn't. The approach taken in this list is to refer to the RFC for the core protocols—IP, ICMP, TCP, and UDP—and refer to books for more-general treatments that include application-layer protocols.

> Comer, Douglas. *Internetworking with TCP/IP, Volume 1.* 3rd Edition. Englewood Cliffs, N.J.: Prentice Hall, 1995. Although not as complete as Rich Stevens's book, Doug Comer's book does an excellent job of fully explaining the core set of TCP/IP protocols. This book is recommended for someone who wants a relatively comprehensive understanding of TCP/IP but wants it as concisely as possible.

> *Internet Protocol.* RFC 791. Prepared for DARPA by USC/ISI. September 1981. The authoritative reference for IP. Many parts of it have been updated by other RFCs over the years, although the bulk of the specification is still in this document.

> Postel, Jon. *Internet Control Message Protocol.* RFC 792. September 1981. The authoritative reference for ICMP. Additional types of messages have been added over the years by other RFCs, but this specification is for the protocol itself and the base set of messages.

> Postel, Jon. *User Datagram Protocol.* RFC 768. August 1980. The authoritative, and still accurate, specification for UDP.

> Stevens, W. Richard. *TCP/IP Illustrated, Volume 1: The Protocols.* Reading, Mass.: Addison-Wesley, 1994. Arguably the most complete reference on TCP/IP. Rich Stevens does an excellent job of clearly and completely explaining all layers of the TCP/IP architecture. The sections on TCP are par-

ticularly good at tying together the many related algorithms. This book is recommended for people who want a total understanding of TCP/IP, including esoteric nuances.

Transport Control Protocol. RFC 793. Prepared for DARPA by USC/ISI. September 1981.
The authoritative reference for TCP. A few options have been added to TCP over the years by other RFCs. Many of the very carefully designed algorithms to deal with controlling and recovering from congestion (for example, slow start, congestion avoidance, and fast retransmit) have only recently been published as RFCs. These algorithms don't introduce interoperability problems with pure RFC 791 implementations, although the algorithms are necessary for the good of the Internet.

A.3 General Routing

All the references listed in this section give more-detailed information about various routing protocols and architecture. No Internet-Drafts or RFCs are listed here because, almost by definition, they are written about a particular protocol. The references here are books that describe the general problem of routing or present a survey of several specific routing protocols.

Halabi, Hassam. *Internet Routing Architectures*. Indianapolis, Ind.: Cisco Press, 1997.
A very practical tutorial on general routing in IP networks with emphasis on products from Cisco Systems.

Huitema, Christian. *Routing in the Internet*. Englewood Cliffs, N.J.: Prentice Hall, 1995.
This book does a good job of giving a broad survey of practical routing issues in the Internet. Some coverage of BGP4 is included. Also included is a fair amount of information about IPv6.

Perlman, Radia. *Interconnections: Bridges and Routers*. Reading, Mass.: Addison-Wesley, 1992.
An excellent reference on the general problem of routing from a computer scientist's perspective. A detailed fundamental

comparison is made between distance vector and link state protocols. A topic covered particularly well is the distribution of link state information in a network along with problems of serial numbers, aging, convergence, and other critical issues. The author does an excellent job of introducing levity into a topic that can be terribly dry.

A.4 BGP

All the references listed in this section give more-detailed information about BGP. With the exception of a couple of earlier references, very few books discuss BGP. As a result, most of the information about BGP is found in RFCs and Internet-Drafts.

Bates, Tony, and Ravi Chandra. *BGP Route Reflection: An Alternative to Full Mesh I-BGP.* RFC 1966. June 1996.
The specification for the route reflection approach to solving the I-BGP scaling problem.

Bates, Tony, Ravi Chandra, Dave Katz, and Yakov Rekhter. *Multiprotocol Extensions for BGP-4.* RFC 2283. February 1998.
The specification for the multiprotocol extensions.

Chandra, Ravi, and John Scudder. *Capabilities Negotiation with BGP-4.* draft-chandra-bgp4-cap-neg. January 1998.
The specification for capabilities negotiation within BGP4.

Chandra, Ravi, Paul Traina, and Tony Li. *BGP Communities Attribute.* RFC 1997. August 1996.
The specification for the community attribute.

Chen, Enke, and John Stewart. *A Framework for Inter-Domain Route Aggregation.* draft-ietf-idr-aggregation-framework. March 1998.
A document describing a disciplined approach to aggregation, both within an AS and between ASs.

Chen, Enke, and Tony Bates. *An Application of the BGP Community Attribute in Multihome Routing.* RFC 1998. August 1996.
A description of a use for the community attribute to ease the

support for multihoming situations when some routes need to be treated as backup.

Heffernan, Andy. *Protection of BGP Sessions via the TCP MD5 Signature Option.* draft-ietf-idr-bgp-tcp-md5. June 1998.
The specification of the MD5 authentication option for TCP. This document includes a discussion of known weaknesses of the approach. On 16 July 1998, the IESG approved RFC publication of this document as a Proposed Standard. After the RFC is published, the document will be accessible only as an RFC and not as an Internet-Draft.

Marques, Pedro, and Francis Dupont. *Use of BGP-4 Multiprotocol Extensions for IPv6 Inter-Domain Routing.* draft-ietf-idr-bgp4-ipv6. February 1998.
The specification for using the multiprotocol extensions to BGP for doing routing of IPv6.

Rekhter, Yakov, and Tony Li. *A Border Gateway Protocol 4 (BGP-4).* draft-ietf-idr-bgp4. February 1998.
The latest publication of the BGP Version 4 specification as an Internet-Draft. This document may eventually become a standard. The changes between RFC 1771 and this Internet-Draft are minor and mostly represent clearing up some inconsistencies and bugs. Two examples are whether a NOTIFICATION should be sent (closing the BGP session) upon receipt of an OPEN message with an unsupported optional parameter and, second, how two routes should be compared if one has a MULTI-EXIT-DISCRIMINATOR attribute and the other doesn't.

Rekhter, Yakov, and Tony Li. *A Border Gateway Protocol 4 (BGP-4).* RFC 1771. March 1995.
The latest publication of the BGP Version 4 specification as an RFC. As of the writing of this text, BGP4 is a Draft Standard protocol. BGP4 may become a Standard at some point in the future, although that seems most likely to happen with the publication of a new RFC.

Stewart, John, and Enke Chen. *Route Aggregation Tutorial.* draft-ietf-idr-aggregation-tutorial. March 1998.
A brief tutorial on what aggregation is and how it works. The intent of this document is to increase aggregation by making sure that the user base is informed.

Traina, Paul. *Autonomous System Confederations for BGP.* RFC 1965. June 1996.
The specification for the confederation approach to solving the I-BGP scaling problem.

Villamizar, Curtis, Ravi Chandra, and Ramesh Govindan. *BGP Route Flap Damping.* draft-ietf-idr-route-damp. May 1998.
The specification for the route flap dampening extension to BGP. This document comes in two versions: ASCII (.txt extension) and PostScript (.ps extension). The PostScript version more effectively conveys the specification details because of the reliance on figures. As of the writing of this text, this Internet-Draft was about to be submitted to the IESG for consideration for Proposed Standard. If approved, the document will be published as an RFC and will cease to be available as an Internet-Draft.

Glossary

access router A router, operated by an ISP, whose primary purpose is to terminate access circuits that go between the ISP and some of its customers.

Adj-RIB-In Each BGP neighbor has an Adj-RIB-In that's used to store the routes learned from that particular BGP neighbor. The specification uses this term as a conceptual explanation; implementers are not required to implement exactly this.

Adj-RIB-Out Each BGP neighbor has an Adj-RIB-Out that's used to store the routes currently being advertised to that particular BGP neighbor. The specification uses this term as a conceptual explanation; implementers are not required to implement exactly this.

aggregate A prefix of some length that is formed by combining several more-specific prefixes.

AS (autonomous system) A collection of routers operated in a coordinated way so that the routers implement the same routing policy; typically operated by a single administrative entity.

AS confederation A single logical AS that is divided into multiple sub-ASs for the sake of I-BGP scalability.

ASN (autonomous system number) A two-byte number that uniquely identifies an AS.

AS-PATH manipulation A change to the contents of the AS-PATH attribute in a way other than the default (for example, extending the length of the AS-PATH).

attribute The basic unit of data used by BGP to describe a prefix (for example, AS-PATH, NEXT-HOP, LOCAL-PREF, and so on).

bit Short for binary digit, the basic unit of binary numbers with a value of either 1 or 0.

BGP (Border Gateway Protocol) The primary inter-domain routing protocol used in the Internet.

BGP peer A router with which a BGP session is established.

BGP session An instance of BGP running between two routers.

broadcast address A special IP address used to send a packet to every IP host on a particular subnetwork.

CIDR (Classless Inter-Domain Routing) A way of referring to IP prefixes. The class (Class A, B, or C) is not implicit based on the value of the leftmost octet; instead, an explicit prefix length is specified.

classful A way of referring to IP prefixes. The class is implicit based on the value of the leftmost octet.

cluster One or more route reflectors and associated route reflector clients in which each of the route reflectors provides reflection for all clients.

common header A 19-octet header that precedes all BGP messages.

community An attribute added to BGP that contains a list of 32-bit community values used to identify a route as belonging to a category of routes, all of which are treated the same with respect to a routing policy.

connectionless A type of protocol (for example, IP) in which no explicit connection is established between two communicating endpoints. Instead, the protocol messages contain enough addressing information to be forwarded through the network without respect to a connection identifier.

connection-oriented A type of protocol in which an explicit connection is established between two communicating endpoints and the protocol messages are forwarded through the network with a connection identifier (for example, the public switched telephone network).

core router A router, operated by an ISP, that has two primary purposes: to serve as a node in the wide-area backbone, terminating relatively high-bandwidth circuits to other core routers, and to connect to local access routers.

cost See metrics.

counting to infinity A failure mode in a DV routing protocol. Each router of two (or more) routers thinks that it reaches a prefix through the other router and continues to pass routing updates with increased metrics until a maximum value is reached.

dampen (also **suppress**) To not advertise a route that has exhibited instability until that route has been stable for a minimum amount of time.

default router A router to which a node forwards a packet if the node doesn't explicitly have a forwarding entry for the destination of the packet.

DHCP (Dynamic Host Configuration Protocol) A protocol used to ease administration of a network of computers by allowing hosts to be dynamically configured from a server that has a database of, for example, address and DNS information.

DNS (Domain Name System) A system used in the Internet that allows nodes to be referenced as alphanumeric names (mnemonics) that are resolvable into numeric IP addresses.

dotted-quad notation A convention for writing IP addresses. Each of the four bytes is written as a separate decimal number, and the four numbers are separated by periods.

DV (distance vector) protocol A broad type of routing protocol in which periodic updates of entire routing tables are sent.

EGP (external gateway protocol) A broad type of routing protocol used to exchange routing information between ASs.

end node A node that is at one of two endpoints with respect to a transport flow.

External BGP (E-BGP) A use of BGP for communicating routing information between routers in different ASs.

flooding algorithm A process of distributing to every node in the network the link state information in an LS routing protocol.

forwarding The process of receiving a packet on an input interface, performing a lookup on the packet's destination address, and copying the packet to the appropriate output interface.

forwarding table The database used to identify the outgoing interfaces for IP prefixes.

FTP (File Transfer Protocol) A protocol used in the Internet to transfer files between computers.

full mesh A topology in which every node in the network is directly connected to every other node. The connections may be physical links or a higher layer abstraction (for example, a full mesh of I-BGP connections).

hold timer A timer that controls the amount of time a BGP speaker should wait before considering its neighbor down.

host A node in a network whose primary purpose is to serve as a user workstation or some kind of server (for example, file server, Web server, and so on).

HTTP (HyperText Transfer Protocol) The protocol used to support the exchange of information used to render a Web page (usually a file formatted according to the Hypertext Markup Language (HTML) standard).

ICMP (Internet Control Message Protocol) The diagnostic part of the network layer used in the Internet for reporting status information, checking connectivity, and so on.

IGP (internal gateway protocol) A broad type of routing protocol used between routers within the same AS.

intermediate node A node through which packets pass between two endpoints of a transport connection.

Internal BGP (I-BGP) A use of BGP between routers within the same AS. It is used to distribute routes within the AS that were learned from some other source (for example, E-BGP, static routes, and so on).

Internet-Draft A document used by the Internet Engineering Task Force and other organizations to publish draft versions of documents that do not have the status of a standard.

IP (Internet Protocol) The network layer protocol used by the Internet.

keepalive A message exchanged from endpoint A to endpoint B so B knows that A is still active. Examples are BGP KEEPALIVEs, link-level keepalives, and IS-IS hellos.

LAN (local area network) A network, such as an Ethernet, that connects computers in a limited geographic area (such as within one building).

Link state (LS) protocols A broad category of routing protocols in which the routing information advertised into the network contains an identifier for the node along with all the other nodes to which it connects.

load balancing The process of distributing traffic between two or more parallel paths to a destination so that the split is relatively even.

load sharing The process of distributing traffic between two or more parallel paths to a destination without qualification as to the evenness of the split.

Loc-RIB The place where routes accepted and selected by a BGP speaker are stored. The specification uses this term as a conceptual explanation; implementers are not required to implement exactly this.

longest match The process of finding an entry in a forwarding or routing table associated with a particular address so that the entry matches more bits in the destination address than any other entry.

loopback interface (also **virtual interface**) A virtual interface in a node that is not associated with any physical circuit or piece of hardware but is considered active as long as the node itself is up.

LSDB (link state database) The collection of all the LSPs about which a router currently knows.

LSP (link state packet) The message that holds the information a router advertises into the network for LS protocols.

mask A string of bits used along with an address to indicate the number of leading bits in the address that correspond with the network part.

MD5 digest A 16-byte value, produced by applying the MD5 algorithm to a message of arbitrary length, that can be used in concert with a secret (password) for cryptographic purposes.

metrics (also **cost**) Values applied to routes and/or links in a routing protocol that are used to select the best route or path—that is, the one having the least cost.

multicast address A special type of address that is used to deliver a packet to all members of a multicast group.

multihoming (1) A host that has multiple interfaces and is connected to more than one network; (2) a network that is connected to more than one ISP.

network (1) A physical infrastructure of links and routers; (2) an IP prefix.

next hop The next node to which a packet should be sent in order to advance the packet closer to the destination.

NOC (network operations center) The facility that performs the operations and management functions for a network.

nontransit service AS1 is said to receive nontransit service from AS2 if, through that connection, AS1 receives connectivity only to AS2 and its customers and not to the entire Internet.

nontransitive A characteristic of a BGP attribute that results in the attribute not being sent past the AS that receives the attribute.

OSI (Open System Interconnect) model The seven-layer model of network protocols of the International Organization for Standardization. From layer 7 down to layer 1, the layers are Application, Presentation, Session, Transport, Internet, Data Link, and Physical.

packet reordering If a packet sent at time *t+1* that is part of a given flow arrives at the destination before a packet sent at time *t* that is part of the same flow, those packets are said to be reordered.

penalty A value that a BGP speaker associates with a route when it is doing route dampening; if that value passes a threshold, the route is suppressed.

ping The common name for the use of the ECHO-REQUEST and ECHO-REPLY ICMP messages to test connectivity between two nodes in a network.

policy routing The ability of a router (and an AS) to control the routes that it accepts from and advertises to other routers (and ASs) as well as the ability to modify the attributes associated with the routes accepted and advertised.

port numbers The value in a transport protocol header that indicates the application process to which a packet is destined.

prefix A group of contiguous bits, from 0 to 32 bits in length, that defines a set of addresses. For example, what used to be called a Class C network would be a 24-bit prefix.

proxy aggregation A type of aggregation in which the AS that performs the aggregation on an address space is not the AS that uses that address space.

recursive lookup If a route lookup results in a next hop that is not directly reachable, a recursive lookup is used to decide how to reach the indirect next hop.

RIB (routing information base) See routing table.

RIP (Routing Information Protocol) A DV routing protocol most often used as a very simple IGP within small networks.

route coloring The act of applying a BGP community attribute with a particular value (such as the "red" value) is said to color the route.

route flapping An instability associated with a prefix in which the route for the prefix may come and go frequently over a short time.

route reflection An approach to I-BGP scaling. Rather than require a full mesh of I-BGP connections, a number of clusters of route reflectors and route reflector clients are used; the route reflectors reflect the routes between their clients and the rest of the AS.

route reflector A BGP speaker that readvertises to other I-BGP neighbors routes learned from its route reflector clients.

route reflector client A standard BGP speaker that advertises its routes to a route reflector and depends on that route reflector to readvertise its routes to the rest of the AS.

route symmetry The route between nodes A and B is said to be symmetric if the path taken from A to B is the same path, except in reverse, as that taken from B to A.

router A computer that typically has two or more interfaces on different networks and provides forwarding of packets between those networks.

router discovery The ability of a node to dynamically discover the routers to which it is adjacent.

routing The process by which a router calculates a forwarding table by using its knowledge of the network taken from local configuration and dynamic routing protocols.

routing registry A database that stores routing policies and can be used for automating the generation of routing policy configurations.

routing table (also **RIB**) A conceptual data structure used to hold routing information.

running Dijkstra See **running SPF**.

running SPF (shortest path first) (also **running Dijkstra**) The process of calculating the shortest path to all destinations by using an LSDB, which includes all the nodes and links in a network along with the metrics associated with those links.

SACK (selective acknowledgment) A feature added to TCP that allows the protocol to acknowledge segments received noncontiguously.

SMTP (Simple Mail Transfer Protocol) The protocol used to transfer electronic mail between computers in the Internet.

suppress See dampen.

TCP (Transmission Control Protocol) The principal reliable transport protocol used in the Internet.

TELNET A protocol used for remote login in the Internet.

third-party next hop The ability of BGP speaker A to advertise a route to BGP speaker B using a NEXT-HOP attribute of router C.

transit service AS1 is said to receive transit service from AS2 if, through that connection, AS1 receives connectivity to the entire Internet and not only AS2 and its customers.

transitive A characteristic of a BGP attribute that results in the attribute being sent past the AS that receives the attribute.

UDP (User Datagram Protocol) The principal unreliable transport protocol used in the Internet.

unicast address The most common type of destination address seen in an IP packet; used to deliver an IP packet to exactly one node.

virtual interface See loopback interface.

well-known attribute A BGP attribute that is required to be known by all BGP implementations.

Index

A

Active state, 32
Address Family Identifier field
   in MP-REACH-NLRI attribute,
    111
   in MP-UNREACH-NLRI
    attribute, 113
   for multiprotocol extensions, 116
Addresses, IP, 6, 12–17
   with CIDR, 28–29
   classes of, 25
   with multihomed subscribers, 71,
    73–74, 80–82
   with TCP, 60–61
Adj-RIB-In, 43–44
Adj-RIB-Out, 43–44
Aggregation
   with AS-PATH, 47
   in CIDR, 27–28
   by ISPs, 84–85
   with multihomed subscribers, 71,
    73, 80–83
   proxy, 29
   and route flapping, 97–98
AGGREGATOR attribute, 52–53
Application layer, 3
AS-CONFED-SET attribute, 96
AS-PATH attribute, 45–47
   for confederations, 96
   with multihomed subscribers,
    83–84
AS-SEQUENCE attribute, 47
AS (autonomous system), 17–18
   confederations, 94–96
Asymmetry, route, 70, 76
ATOMIC-AGGREGATE attribute,
   52

Attribute Flags field, 38, 40
Attribute Length field
   for community attribute, 102
   in UPDATE message, 40
Attribute Type field, 38–40
Attribute Value field, 40
Attributes
   AGGREGATOR, 52–53
   AS-CONFED-SET, 96
   AS-PATH, 45–47
   ATOMIC-AGGREGATE, 52
   CLUSTER-LIST, 94
   community, 99–108
   LOCAL-PREF, 50–52
   MP-REACH-NLRI, 110–113
   MP-UNREACH-NLRI, 113–114
   MULTI-EXIT-DISCRIMINATOR,
    48–50
   NEXT-HOP, 47–48
   ORIGIN, 44–45
   ORIGINATOR-ID, 93–94
Authentication
   in OPEN message, 36
   TCP MD5, 108–109
Automatic backup routes,
   106–108
Autonomous system (AS),
   17–18
   confederations, 94–96

B

Backup routes, 106–108
BGP connections, establishing,
   31–33
Best Current Practice (BCP) RFC,
   118
BGP Identifier field, 35

131

♦ THE ADDISON–WESLEY NETWORKING BASICS SERIES

Focused and Concise Hands-On Guides for Networking Professionals

The Addison-Wesley Networking Basics Series is a set of concise, hands-on guides to today's key computer networking technologies and protocols. Each volume in the series covers a focused topic, presenting the steps required to implement and work with specific technologies and tools in network programming, administration, and security. Providing practical, problem-solving information, these books are written by practicing professionals who have mastered complex network challenges.

0-201-37951-1

0-201-37956-2

0-201-61584-3

0-201-37924-4

0-201-60448-5

0-201-37957-0

0-201-43320-6

0-201-65773-2

Please visit our Web site at
http://www.aw.com/cseng/networkingbasics/
for more information on these titles.